THE HANDGUN GUIDE FOR WOMEN

© 2015 Quarto Publishing Group USA Inc.
Text © 2015 Tara Dixon Engel
Photography © 2015 Tara Dixon Engel (unless otherwise noted)

First published in 2015 by Zenith Press, an imprint of Quarto Publishing Group USA Inc., 400 First Avenue North, Suite 400, Minneapolis, MN 55401 USA.
Telephone: (612) 344-8100 Fax: (612) 344-8692

quartoknows.com
Visit our blogs at quartoknows.com

Zenith Press titles are also available at discounts in bulk quantity for industrial or sales-promotional use. For details contact the Special Sales Manager at Quarto Publishing Group USA Inc., 400 First Avenue North, Suite 400, Minneapolis, MN 55401 USA.

10 9 8 7 6 5 4 3 2 1

ISBN: 978-0-7603-4853-6

Acquiring Editor: Elizabeth Demers
Project Manager: Caitlin Fultz
Art Director: James Kegley
Layout: Kazuko Collins

Front cover photo by Layne English

Printed in China

THE *HANDGUN* GUIDE *FOR WOMEN*

SHOOT STRAIGHT, SHOOT SAFE, and CARRY with CONFIDENCE

TARA DIXON ENGEL

ZENITH
PRESS

To Matt and the Engel family—who taught me the beauty, tradition, and honor of hunting; to Lt. Col. Mike Jackson, USAF (Ret.)—who gave me the courage to become a pistol-packin' mama; to Evan English and the gang at Olde English Outfitters—who gave me a chance, treated me like "one of the guys," and showed me true faith in action; to my wonderful, courageous husband, John Falldorf, whose patience, wisdom, support, and kindness (and sense of humor) never waver—and who never yells at me when he finds ammunition in the washer or the freezer; to my son, Michael, who makes me proud every day. You are a great shot . . . and are becoming an even greater man. I am truly blessed.

—Tara Dixon Engel

CONTENTS

THE FIGHTING YOUNG LIBERAL

I didn't start out as a "gun girl." In fact, I was never around guns as a child, except for a rusty old .22 rifle that collected dust on a bookcase in my father's den. I don't know if it had ever been fired, and I'm pretty sure its only real defensive use would have been to swing it at the head of an unsuspecting intruder. As a little girl, I picked it up once or twice, just to see what it felt like, but I never pulled the trigger or even thought to look around for ammunition. The gun didn't scare me but it also didn't interest me. Although my parents weren't especially anti-gun, I don't recall discussing the Second Amendment or gun rights during our family dinners.

Still, my childhood and young adult years were spent nursing a distinct distaste for guns, hunters, and anyone who claimed to be a shooter. I bought into the popular media's portrayal of gun owners as overweight redneck males with a loaded gun in one hand, a six-pack of beer cradled in the other, and no respect for life, human or otherwise.

Admittedly, my only early experience with guns or hunters was an arm's-length interaction with a neighbor who regularly trespassed on our property while rabbit hunting. We lived on six-plus acres that sat adjacent to his fifteen acres of woods and fields. My parents owned a variety of cats and the occasional dog, not to mention having two daughters who spent a great deal of time outdoors, so they were understandably wary of this fellow who would nod patiently as my father pointed out that he was trespassing, only to turn around and do it again a couple weeks later!

So perhaps I was somewhat justified in my early view of hunters and guns.

All that changed in my early twenties, when I fell in love with a young man whose passion was duck hunting. Matt and his family lived on an eighty-three-acre farm where they hunted not only ducks, but deer, rabbit, and squirrels as well.

Tom Reichner/Shutterstock

Our first Christmas together, he presented me with a twelve-gauge single-shot Harrington & Richardson shotgun—and I cried like a baby. Okay, I had been secretly hoping for an engagement ring, but that's not why I cried. I cried because I rightly interpreted his gift as an indication that he wanted me to share his interests and, in so doing, his life. It was almost as good as a ring and just as symbolic. As I hoisted that gun to my shoulder, I bid a final farewell to the shadow of that "fighting young liberal" who had once passionately declared "people should hunt hunters!"

Indeed, I responded to his gift with both enthusiasm and determination—and immediately began learning to shoot. I made my share of mistakes, but Matt was careful to stress safety at all times. Thankfully, because of that, I lived to tell the tale of my errors, and so did those around me. Eventually, I was shooting pheasants, ducks, and squirrels with the best of them. My crowning achievement was a fourteen-point buck with a split brow point, taken on my by-then husband's family farm in the late 1980s. I still have the rack, and I still smile as I remember that hunt and the many lessons of that chilly autumn day.

It had been a typical prehunt morning at the farm. The family (consisting of six boys and two parents) gathered in the large 1820s kitchen to plot the day's hunt. Pop put the coffeepot on, and the boys argued among themselves about who would "push" and who would wait patiently for the deer to come their way (which, more often than not, didn't happen). The laughter and debate drifted into the bedroom upstairs where I was sleeping, and I grudgingly wandered into the kitchen, bleary-eyed and silently cursing anyone who could be so jovial at 5:30 a.m. Matt handed me a cup of coffee and asked if I wanted to go to the woods.

I mumbled a groggy no. "Anyway, I didn't bring my gun or my long johns. All I have is my license and a jacket," I said, trying to shake the cobwebs from my mind.

He shook his head. "No problem—we can fix you up with the clothes. You can borrow Mom's boots and gun. If you want to go, we can get you suited up." I noticed that peripheral discussion had stopped and the other brothers were eyeing me curiously. One of the older boys scoffed. "I don't think she's cut out to be a deer hunter!"

"Nah, but wouldn't it be funny if she borrowed our clothes and our gun . . . and then went out and shot 'the big one'?" someone suggested. Everyone laughed. Someone else piped up, "She's never even been deer hunting before. Even if she saw one, she'd get buck fever and freeze up. It happens to everyone the first time."

Having been raised among mostly females, I was still getting used to this strange male ritual of showing your affection for someone by beating them up verbally. I bristled at their laughter and turned to my husband. "Yes . . . on second thought, I *do* want to hunt today."

Matt began assembling my hunting gear as the rest of the boys returned to a heated discussion of where the deer would be bedded down, based on the phase of the moon—and whether anyone would catch a glimpse of the glorious fourteen-point buck that had become near-legend on Telegraph Mills Farm.

Once again, the discussion drifted into the ludicrous idea that Tara—who had never hunted deer before—Tara, a *girl*, wearing borrowed long johns, borrowed boots, and toting a borrowed gun, might actually bag one. Again there was laughter.

I smiled indulgently and gave the boys an anatomically impossible suggestion (in the most ladylike way possible) as I followed Matt out into the frigid darkness. Shivering, I watched my breath turn to ice crystals in the cold morning air. I was already missing my soft, warm bed as hubby set me up on a folding stool at the base of an old oak tree. "Just sit still and wait," he instructed. "You know what to do if you see one. I'll head to the north field and see if I can push him toward you." I chattered a reply and tucked my face into a borrowed scarf—and waited.

I tried to sit as still as I could, knowing that deer are far from stupid. Indeed, if you didn't skew the playing field with salt licks or corn (something my husband's family was adamantly against), the deer usually got the better of you. I wasn't expecting much as I shivered on my chilly perch at the base of a natural amphitheater. I took a deep breath and tried to pretend that my feet weren't already starting to go numb from the cold.

Then it happened—I heard the sound of pounding hooves directly up the hill above me, as if a horse had just galloped across the field and was crossing the fence line and heading down into the amphitheater. I didn't immediately understand what I was hearing. Then came the crunch of leaves and twigs as something moved through the woods toward me— something big. And, suddenly, there he was—Bambi's father—the king of the forest. Holy crap!

Standing broadside about twenty yards from me was the most beautiful animal I had ever seen. Majestic, regal, and with its head cocked slightly, staring straight at me. I gasped and buck fever crept in. "I can't shoot this beautiful animal," I thought. "There's just no way." Then, just as suddenly, the voices of my brothers-in-law elbowed their way into my mind and erased all hint of buck fever. "Hey wouldn't it be funny if Tara shot a deer?" I recalled them saying. "Nah, it'll never happen." "Tara? Shoot a deer? Bwa-haha-hahahahaha."

BANG! The shot startled even me, despite the fact that it was my finger pulling the trigger.

The deer stepped sideways, glanced at me again, and took off running. "Well, I tried," I thought as I lowered the twelve-gauge, set the safety with shaky fingers, and leaned the gun against the tree. My heart was racing and adrenaline was coursing through my body. I kicked myself for not aiming more carefully, especially since the deer gave me a massive target by standing sideways. A few minutes later, I heard more feet pounding across the field and into the woods. These were most certainly human.

"Hey," Matt shouted, "did you get him?" I shook my head no, as he trotted down the hill to the spot where Bambi's dad had been standing.

"Really? You missed him?" he asked. I nodded. "Then I guess he was bleeding when he ran down here?"

What? Had I really hit him?

Indeed I had. In fact, when Matt and his brothers finally tracked him down, we discovered I had blown out both lungs. But this was a tough old buck, and he hadn't lived so long by giving up easily.

I was at least as shocked and startled by my achievement as the brothers were. The grand old buck that had been glimpsed and missed and spoken of in hushed tones for so many seasons had finally been felled at the hands of a novice—and a girl novice, no less.

In the end, about all that was salvageable from the old buck was his sprawling rack. We ate the backstraps that night and they were barely edible.

Opposite page: This vintage photo reflects my jubilation when I bagged the big one. I did not, however, toss it over my shoulder! *Everett Collection/Shutterstock*

A typical tenderloin backstrap is something akin to the finest Wagu beef. It is melt-in-your-mouth perfection. But Bambi's dad had been around a long, long time, and he was tough, not only in character but in consistency. We had the rest of the meat ground into hamburger—but even that was substandard.

Still, it was the story that counted. And, despite the merciless teasing I had endured from my brothers-in-law, the whole incident became a told-and-retold tale—and a point of family pride.

And, yes, it has been a very useful tool through the years when I needed to put a doubting male in his place. Sometimes, in my classes or behind the gun counter, I get a mildly disgusted look from the occasional unevolved male who cannot believe he is being assisted or taught by a woman.

"So, have you ever actually hunted?" is the inevitable, slightly snarky, question. I nod slowly. "Well, yeah, a little," I say, "mostly pheasant and duck, some squirrel, rabbit, a few pigeons for target practice . . . and then there was the fourteen-point buck with the split brow point that I took a few years back." That usually silences them and even generates a grudging nod of respect.

I tell this story not to pat myself on the back. Indeed, I bagged that deer through pure teamwork—and I was the *least* active person on the team. Matt did the pushing, then tracked the deer, and then he and his brothers dragged it up the hill and back to the farmhouse. Me? I was in the bathroom getting sick to my stomach because of all the excess adrenaline!

No, I tell this story because it contains a number of lessons I hope to impart in this book:

- **It shows that you can change your attitude.** If you fear guns or hate hunters, that is certainly your right, but at least take the time to get to know real people, not caricatures. And take time to learn about guns before you assume they are inherently evil.

- Although Matt eventually became my ex-husband many years later, I will always be grateful for his careful instruction in gun usage and, most of all, in gun safety. He did it the right way, and, to this day, I still recall that the first thing I did after firing the deer slug at Bambi's dad was to snap on the safety and set the gun down. That lesson of safe gun handling is one we passed along to our son (who was probably eight or nine the first time his father took him squirrel hunting). **Bottom line: if you are taught to respect firearms and use them safely, you will be far less likely to do something stupid.**

- **If you choose to hunt with, carry, or even own a gun, you take on a great responsibility.** For hunters, you make a tacit agreement with God and nature to not allow animals to suffer needlessly. I have met hunters over the years who made me physically sick by bragging about exceeding the limits and burying the evidence. I shoot for food, as Matt's family taught me to do. And I follow the laws.

  For those who don't hunt but want to carry a firearm, the responsibility is even greater. Hunting happens seasonally. Carrying happens almost every day. You are required to be ever aware of where your gun is and where you are (and, ladies, if you carry a gun in your purse—as we will discuss in chapter 9—that need for awareness is compounded). And, again, you must follow the laws—even if you don't agree with them. If you don't carry but you plan to keep a gun for home protection, you are still obligated to not only store it safely (*very* safely if you have children or grandchildren) but to also become competent in its use and maintenance. I tend to favor analogies between guns and cars. Both are tools that can be used—and abused. Both require training to use safely. Both require maintenance in order to stay safe and to perform at optimum levels. And the use of both, like it or not, is tied to government regulations and approvals.

- Whether you are hunting or defending yourself, using a firearm creates the likelihood that you may take the life of another living thing. I was sick for two hours after shooting my trophy buck. Yes, I had shot ducks and pheasants before, but nothing that looked so much like a pet—nothing that shared mammal status with me. Believe me, it made a difference. It rattled me. Imagine how much more disconcerting it is to shoot another human being, even one that is intent on harming you or your family. Several years ago, after a decade as a single mom, I was fortunate to meet and marry a wonderful man who had spent almost three decades of his life in law enforcement. Through John, I have come to understand the emotional challenges that accompany shooting another human being. While it is always your last resort, you don't always have time to make a measured judgment call (and, in fact, if you do have the luxury of time, you should be running the other direction rather than pondering the ramifications of taking a life). The bottom line is that before you even consider buying a gun for personal protection, you need to understand that its purpose—the reason you are buying it—is to kill someone who wants to kill you. Period. In later chapters we will discuss those folks (frequently women, in my experience) who say "I just want a gun so I can scare an intruder." We call those people victims.

As I moved into my thirties and forties, I got busy raising a child and eventually gave up most of my hunting (though I recently ventured back into the fold because I love the taste of well-prepared wild game). And throughout those years, it never occurred to me to consider buying or learning to use a handgun. Indeed, I had only ever used shotguns and rifles. Once, when I was in my early thirties, Matt had handed me a large .38 revolver. With no offer of ear protection, no explanation of how a handgun worked, and no guidance on grip or stance, he simply said, "Point it at that tree and pull the trigger." I did so. I don't recall which startled me more, the recoil or the noise, but I handed him the gun and said "never again."

And for years I stuck by that declaration. Indeed, just knowing that the shiny black Smith & Wesson sat on the top shelf of our closet made me uneasy. Although a sprawling gun case in the den housed over a dozen shotguns and rifles, I didn't have the same wariness about them. Even today, I don't fully understand that disconnect—both types of firearms operate essentially the same way and produce the same results. But I was absolutely certain that a revolver was capable of discharging on its own and creating death and destruction with little or no human assistance.

It was years later, when a friend bought me a concealed carry class for Christmas, that I began to discover the folly in my thinking. As I progressed from fearful student to concealed handgun license holder to competent shooter to NRA-certified instructor and firearms salesperson, I gained a progressively better understanding of what guns can—and cannot—do. I lost my irrational fear of handguns and replaced it with respect and appreciation. I have learned to like guns and to enjoy using them in a variety of sporting venues. More important, I understand their defensive value to the female of the species. In a world where men almost always have a weight and muscle advantage over women, handguns level the playing field. I like that. At five feet four inches and 125 pounds, I would have a tough time running from or physically overcoming a taller, heavier male assailant. But I can aim and pull a trigger with the best of them—and it's likely I'll be able to do so for many, many more years. I take comfort in that and in the fact that, although I can't get taller, faster, or even much stronger, I can always improve my aim and comfort level with any given firearm.

This book grew out of the many questions I once had and those I regularly encounter in my classes and at the gun shop. Women often approach the gun counter timidly, apologizing in advance for

The Second Amendment guarantees the right of the people to keep and bear arms. And the writings of our founding fathers confirm that this is *not* just for a "well-regulated militia." *Sean Locke Photography/Shutterstock*

their ignorance. While all the salespeople in our shop are patient and understanding, I think it often benefits women (or new shooters of any gender) to be guided by a "kinder, gentler" individual.

It also helps when I tell my students and customers that none of their doubts or questions are stupid. They are, in some cases, a product of paying too much attention to the national media or watching too many shoot-'em-up TV shows and movies. It just doesn't work the way Hollywood (or, too often, the nightly news) likes to portray.

Or perhaps your questions simply stem from ignorance—and I mean a lack of practical experience, not stupidity. Ignorance can be cured with education (stupid is terminal). This book aims to provide that education, along with some good stories, real-life experiences, step-by-step instruction, and a few carefully directed barbs at those folks who not only choose to remain ignorant about handguns, but demand that I be governed by their ignorance.

I have no issue with people who don't like or don't choose to own guns. That is their right. My right, however, as guaranteed by the Second Amendment to the Constitution, is the right to keep and bear arms. My *responsibility* is to do so in a manner that is safe, competent, vigilant to the rights of others, and always willing to share knowledge and information.

I have worked hard to do and be all of the above (and it is an ongoing process). This book is a step toward helping you do likewise.

CHAPTER 1

WHAT GUNS ARE— AND AREN'T

My first experience with a handgun was short and sweet. I pointed my then-husband's heavy black Smith & Wesson revolver at my "target"—a sprawling old maple tree—and struggled to pull the trigger. After a few seconds of tugging, I was shocked by the tremendous roar and a certainty that the gun was going to fly backwards out of my hand and whack me in the head. Shocked and rattled, I quickly handed the revolver back to my hubby.

"No thanks—I'll stick with shotguns," I said defiantly.

And I did. For years.

That one negative experience taught me a lot. It taught me that all handguns are painful to shoot. It taught me that they are ungainly in the hand and almost impossible to control. It taught me that I could never learn to master something that unpleasant and ergonomically awkward. Yes, my first encounter with pistols taught me a lot—all of it wrong.

But I wouldn't find that out for a very long time, precisely *because* my first foray into pistol shooting had been so unstructured and impromptu. Matt had always been very good about proper instruction in firearms safety, so this was atypical of him. I think he probably knew I wouldn't like the gun to begin with. (I had always been pretty vocal about keeping my distance from pistols.) This was, I suspect, a cursory exercise on his part—give her the gun, let her shoot it once, put it away, and drop the subject. At least then, if I ever needed it and he was not at home, I would know where to point and what to pull. Beyond that, he offered no particular instruction and no guidance on how to grip or how to stand. There was just noise and a tongue of flame leaping from the muzzle.

Unfortunately, that experience only heightened my nightmares about the heavy black revolver hiding on the top shelf of our bedroom closet. I would periodically creep into the closet and pile things on top of it, expecting—what? That it was going to climb down and come find me? That it might spontaneously begin firing (as if a pile of clothing would prevent that)? In truth, I have no idea what I expected or feared. I just knew that—like so many things in life—I didn't understand it, so it scared me. I even took to hiding it in a dresser drawer when Matt and I were fighting, not because he had ever used it, mentioned it, or even looked at it in a threatening manner. But, somehow, I perceived its very presence as a threat. Somehow, that revolver would call to him when he was most vulnerable, and he would be helpless to resist. It was there. It was handy. And he would eventually avail himself of it—right?

With that logic, I suppose I should have hidden the butcher knives, baseball bats, hammers, chainsaws, and, oh yeah, the fifteen assorted twelve- and twenty-gauge shotguns hanging on the wall in the den.

I didn't say my fears were logical—only that they were very compelling. And today I hear those same fears echoed by women on a regular basis. I have to remind myself—lest I silently cringe at their concerns—that I once nursed identical phobias.

So—what changed? I'd like to say the passage of time and the blossoming of wisdom and maturity. I'd *like* to say that, but mostly it was the persistence of my buddy Mike, many years later, who decided that I needed to go target shooting with him. He had a couple of .22 rifles and I'd always been comfy with a long gun, so I tagged along and had a great time. A state-of-the-art indoor range had recently opened nearby in Vandalia, and this was my first experience shooting indoors. The facility was clean, family run, and staffed by both women and men. I liked that, and I immediately felt comfortable. That same facility also rented out handguns and rifles by the hour. I had never heard of such a thing, but Mike insisted that we come back and rent pistols. I sighed. Maybe in a controlled environment I could overcome my paranoia. Maybe.

This time I did it right: I started slow and simple. The next visit to the range, Mike brought his .22 LR single-action revolver, and we rented a Walther P22 semi-automatic pistol, trading the two guns

New shooters should try revolvers and semi-automatics as they decide what suits their needs, wallet, and comfort.

back and forth. I mostly shot the revolver, except when Mike handed me the already-loaded P22 and said, "Just flip the safety off and you're ready to shoot." I was grateful for his assistance because the internal workings of that little semi-automatic completely mystified me.

The revolver, on the other hand, was simple to load and simple to shoot. And, much to my joy, there was no painful recoil jarring my hands and very little noise jarring my ears. (Of course, this time I had on ear and eye protection.)

I enjoyed shooting both Mike's revolver and the rental gun and was pleased to discover that .22 LR (which stands for "long rifle") in most gun designs is a comfortable round to shoot. The quality of my shooting left something to be desired, but at least I was hitting the target—well, most of the time.

So, why did I hate my hubby's old black Smith & Wesson .38 Special but love shooting the .22s? Well, for starters, they fire two very different ammunition rounds. A .22 Long Rifle is a small, light piece of ammo whose primary use is target and varmint shooting (varmints being those mostly rural nuisances, ranging from raccoons to possums). A .38 carries a larger, heavier projectile (a.k.a. bullet) and more powerful powder charge

Gun Girl Tip #1

The gun you take to the range may be relatively quiet, but remember that the guy in the shooting stall beside you may be firing a Smith & Wesson 500 or a full-sized 1911 .45 ACP (Automatic Colt Pistol)—both very large and loud guns. It took me several years and many visits to the range before I stopped jumping reflexively every time a loud shot caught me off guard. And—don't tell anyone— sometimes I still jump!

(the stuff that forces the bullet out of the gun). For many years, .38s were the caliber of choice for most police departments, while .22s are often the subject of great debate among shooters as to whether they should ever be used for defensive purposes. Later in this book, we will tackle that topic, but for now, suffice it to say that I had taken my first tenuous step toward overcoming my fear of handguns. It was a baby step, to be certain, but the next time Mike said, "Let's go to the range," I responded with enthusiasm.

I had learned my first—and a very important—lesson on my path toward becoming a gun girl: all guns are *not* created equal. Like cars or shoes or anything else designed for consumers, there are vast differences between models, and, truly, there is something out there for just about anyone.

So, what about you? Chances are, if you are female, you are probably going to shy away from the loud, heavy, high-caliber models at first. And that's fine. But before you write them off completely, make sure you understand the relationship between weight, size, and caliber.

In the beginning, I wanted nothing to do with a big gun. The bigger it was, the more it scared me, in part because the Smith & Wesson I had fired at my husband's urging had been a full-sized revolver. At my level of understanding, a big gun was automatically (a) heavy and therefore unpleasant to hold aloft, (b) loud and scary, and (c) punishing on the hands.

What I didn't grasp was that size was only a small part of the equation, and, in fact, I wasn't even doing the math properly. I was not factoring in how I held the gun, how I stood while shooting, the type of gun it

Guns come in all sizes, from the large, heavy Desert Eagle from Magnum Research to the pocket-friendly LC9 by Ruger.

was, or even the caliber of the gun. Heck, in the beginning, I didn't even understand that every gun is "chambered" for a different caliber of ammunition. The gun you are shooting may have a gun barrel whose bore (the inside of the barrel) has a diameter designed for .22 LR ammunition, or maybe it's built for 9mm rounds, or perhaps .45 ACP. Each of those bullet sizes is different, and a gun built for one will not fire the other, except in rare cases where a gun is designed to have interchangeable barrels—or with certain, very specific calibers that are close enough in circumference and case design that they can be used interchangeably. But we'll tackle those in chapter 7. For now, just understand that every barrel is bored for a specific sized cartridge.

So, yes, size does matter, ladies. But not just the size of the gun itself: the size of the ammo—and the size/amount of the powder charge inside the cartridge case—also play a major role in whether, or how much, the gun hurts your hand.

The truth is that a smaller gun will almost always be more painful to shoot. In my work as a gun salesperson, I am ever surprised when female customers gravitate to small firearms. Not just gravitate, mind you, but actively rebuff any effort to put a larger gun in their hands. I often get a suspicious look when I try to explain that they would probably enjoy

Guns come in all shapes, sizes, and calibers. To enjoy shooting, you must select the combination that works for you.

shooting a larger gun more. The ingrained logic seems to be: small size equals small boom and small kick. Not so.

Now, if you combine small size *and* small caliber, you will get a somewhat modified recoil. But, even then, don't underestimate the tradeoffs that come with portability. One of the least appealing guns I ever owned was a .22 Magnum pocket pistol made by North American Arms. It was a cool-looking little revolver that fit absolutely anywhere. Had I wanted to drop it into my underwear, I could have done so with very little discomfort. Unfortunately, it was so small—and, at .22 Magnum, just powerful enough—that the stupid gun would not stay in my hand when firing, no matter how I held it. In fact, it was so small that just keeping my fingers away from the barrel during firing was a challenge! Although .22 Magnum is a slightly more powerful round than .22 LR, it's still pretty tame. But that miniature revolver delivered a surprisingly potent kick and accompanying muzzle flip.

Conversely, if you took a .22 LR or a .22 Magnum round and dropped it into a full-sized revolver or semi-automatic with a four-inch barrel, you would barely notice the recoil.

My students often cringe when I invite them to shoot my Sig Sauer 1911 .45 ACP. The gun is a full-sized, steel-framed 1911—a classic firearm built to almost the same specs as John Browning first designed it in, yes, 1911.

With a five-inch barrel and beefy grip, it is a big gun. New shooters often hesitate at the idea of firing a powerful round from a large-framed gun. But I have yet to have a student who fired that awesome piece of workmanship and did *not* say, in essence, "Wow, that was a lot different than I thought it would be! I like it!"

Once again, size matters! A .45 ACP round in a tiny frame is devastating on the hand. But a .45 ACP round in a full-sized frame is not only reasonably comfortable but amazingly accurate, no matter your experience level.

My students are routinely shocked to find that their hits are all over the target when shooting a .22 LR but become nicely patterned in a neat little bunch when shooting a full-sized .45 ACP. Weight not only helps diminish recoil, it also helps with accuracy (as does a longer barrel).

For many years, .45s were the caliber of choice in the military. They are, today, one of the primo personal defense rounds as well as a popular option for range and competitive shooting. Shooting a .45 ACP well *consistently* requires practice and focus, but it is a very versatile and rewarding round to shoot. And ladies, the men nod respectfully when you hoist and fire a 1911 at the range.

Gun Girl Tip #2

Every gun is built to chamber and shoot a particular size (or caliber) of ammo. The power of that round of ammo—combined with the size of the gun—helps to determine how much or how little it will kick your hand (recoil) when you shoot it.

But, as a beginner, you will want to work your way up to a .45. There's no shame in starting off with a .22 LR or a .380 and perfecting your proficiency over time. That's how I did it!

The first gun I carried was a Walther P22, a cute little .22 LR pistol that rode in my purse until I felt sufficiently at ease with a Springfield XD 9mm. The XD was a great gun—one I still use today with my classes and for home defense—but it was a full-sized gun, and, with sixteen rounds of 9mm ammo tucked into it, it was heavy. What was perfect on the range was definitely not perfect in my purse (just ask my chiropractor).

And, by the way, there is no *one* "perfect gun." Each model and caliber is intended for a specific purpose—concealed carry, home defense, target shooting, hunting, etc. And it is very rare to find one model that serves multiple purposes. We'll tackle that in more detail later, but for now, remember that once you become a shooter, you will likely be consumed by the desire to own and shoot multiple guns—and then you will finally "get it."

Gun Girl Tip #3

Weight is your friend. A big, heavy gun, whether it is chambered for .22 LR, 9mm, or .45 ACP, will always deliver a more comfortable shooting experience than a small, lightweight gun chambered for the same caliber. Important to know when you are shopping for the "perfect gun."

I still recall the beginner's class where I listed the numerous reasons one might own a gun and the types of guns that would be appropriate to each reason. At the back of the room sat a female student, arms folded, face radiating a desire to be just about *anywhere* but in that classroom. I found out later that her husband had insisted she take the class since he owned multiple guns and wanted her to be competent to use them if he was not at home.

"You may wonder why gun owners usually have more than one gun," I lectured, ignoring the obvious displeasure of my student. "It isn't because we're all crazed anarchists—it is simply because each gun has a specific purpose, and most guns are only truly effective when they are being used for that purpose. A concealed carry gun is rarely a comfortable range gun, a home defense gun is not usually concealable, a target pistol is not a gun you would tote around for defensive purposes, and so on."

At the back of the class, I caught a strange expression creeping into the eyes of my disinterested student. It was like a light bulb had switched on over her head, and her face was suddenly bathed in the glow of comprehension. She grinned broadly and piped up, "Oh my gosh, I get it now—they're like shoes!" Every lady in the class laughed and nodded, while the men smiled politely and looked a tad confused.

But it was one of the best analogies I've ever heard, and I still use it in all my beginner classes. You don't wear gym shoes to the prom, or flip-flops to run a race, or high heels to muck out a stall. *Could you?* Well, yes, of course. *But that is not the intended purpose of that particular shoe.* Same with guns.

I must add that my unhappy student went on to shoot all the guns available to her in the intro class (from .22 LR up to .45 ACP)—and shoot very well, too. Several weeks later, she showed up, beaming, at the gun counter—with a happy hubby in tow—to purchase her first pistol, a full-sized 9mm Springfield XD. I suspect it was not her last.

One of my favorite carry guns is the .380 Sig Sauer P238. It is light enough to carry but heavy enough for a comfortable shoot.

CHAPTER SUMMARY

- Every gun is chambered for a specific size/caliber of ammunition.

- How the gun "kicks" (recoils) will depend on the size and power/energy of the ammunition, relative to the size of the gun.

- Big guns are typically easier on the hands to shoot because the size and weight of the piece helps to absorb/redistribute some of the recoil.

- .22 LR and .22 Magnum are relatively "light" rounds of ammunition (suitable primarily for target practice and ridding the land of varmints—the four-legged variety).

- .38 Special is a midrange round (between .22 and .45) that was once the round of choice for police departments.

- .45 ACP is a heavy, powerful round formerly used by the military, now used in personal defense, range shooting, and competitive venues.

- Every gun has a specific purpose for which it was created. When you buy a gun, you must consider *why* you want the gun and select a firearm that is appropriate to that purpose.

CHAPTER 2

GUNS AND GALS —THEY *DO* MIX

I'd love to say women and men are the same when it comes to handling firearms. But if I did, I'd be lying. The two sexes are built differently (thank heavens), and they often approach life differently, whether by nature or by nurture.

I've never, ever had a male student or customer tell me he "only wants a gun to scare people" or that he "can't imagine actually shooting someone." Are there men who feel that way? Of course there are, but they probably don't buy guns.

A woman, however, may see the value of owning a firearm without fully making that emotional leap into actually using it. She may see it as a deterrent but not necessarily as a tool.

Owning a gun with the hope that it will scare someone is the personal defense equivalent of buying a fire extinguisher and then watching helplessly as your home burns to the ground. Tools have a purpose in your life. If you don't use them for their assigned purpose, they might as well be expensive paperweights.

Not every female or beginning shooter grapples with the question "Could I use this gun against an assailant?" but many, if not most, pause and wonder. As an NRA instructor and an avid shooter, I used to confidently tell my classes that I could and would shoot someone who was threatening me or my family. But, in my heart of hearts, I knew I had never been put to the test—not even a little. I didn't really know how I would react, whether I would remember my training or panic and do something stupid.

I got a glimpse of an answer several years ago. I was sharing a house with another single mom of a teenaged boy. We were in a decent part of town and had never had any reason to question the safety of our neighborhood.

Gun Girl Tip #4

Always remember that professional criminals are pretty good at discerning genuine threats. They will likely be able to quickly determine whether or not you will pull the trigger—and the longer you delay, the more certain they are that you are not a threat. And, as far as "scaring" them goes, if you make your living breaking into other people's homes and stealing their stuff, you probably don't scare very easily!

One night about midnight, someone began pounding on our heavy, windowless front door. My housemate and I emerged from our rooms at roughly the same time, making a beeline toward the door. The difference, of course, is that I was carrying a loaded Springfield XD-9. She reached for the front door handle as I shouted "No!" and motioned her away from the door.

"Who is it?" I yelled, bracing my shoulder against the door frame and summoning my best "deep, scary tone."

"Help me! You have to let me in," came a panicked female voice from the other side of the door. "My boyfriend is drunk and he's trying to beat me up. He's coming after me! I think he's going to kill me! You have to let me in!"

"Okay . . . okay, it's all right," I said. "Where is he right now?"

"I don't know but he's after me, please let me in! I need to call the police," came the tearful plea.

I continued to shake my head no to my housemate and asked her to call 911. Glancing out a side window, I expected to see a drunken maniac racing up the sidewalk toward the house, but the street was empty. Our frantic visitor huddled beneath the awning of our front porch, still crying and pleading. At this point I began questioning my own actions and words. *What if I am doing the wrong thing? What if this guy shows up and kills her right on my front porch? How can I be so heartless as to not let this poor thing into my home? What kind of terrible person am I?*

My rattled mind was playing tricks on me as I fought to stay calm.

"It's okay," I yelled, in a semicomforting tone through the door. "We are calling 911 and the police are on their way. I'm holding a loaded 9mm, and if your boyfriend tries to hurt you, I *will* shoot him. Okay?"

"Uh . . . okay," came the suddenly composed response.

I was already walking through the various scenarios in my mind: where I would stand, where I would shoot, under what circumstances

I would shoot—I felt like my head was going to explode. In reality, these were things I should have thought about long before now, but I hadn't taken the time to ponder worst-case scenarios. And now I was dealing with one!

My housemate stood nearby explaining the situation to the police, and I stayed beside the front door, gun in hand, finger extended along the frame, fighting to control my ragged breathing and pounding heart.

I remember wondering what was really going on, whether the girl's rampaging beau was going to try to bash down our front door and, vaguely, whether there even *was* a rampaging beau. But mostly, as the thoughts flashed through my head, I felt fuzzy and my hands shook uncontrollably.

We shouted to her that the police were on their way, at which point we noticed she was no longer standing on the front stoop but was pacing on the path that led out to the sidewalk. And she was talking on her cell phone! Even in my adrenalized state, I was puzzled as to why she needed to get into our house in order to call the police if she was carrying a cell phone the whole time!

The police pulled up in front of our home and began chatting with the now-calm young lady.

My friend and I watched and waited in the house, expecting someone to let us know the outcome, but within a few minutes, the cop car was gone and so was our frantic visitor.

My experience with a potential home invasion taught me that I could keep my cool in a high-stress situation, although I felt anything but cool as the situation unfolded. *Randall Vermillion/Shutterstock*

We sat up for a while, too shaky and unnerved to sleep, half expecting the crazed woman to return. When I finally went to bed, I slipped my gun into the bookcase near my head and eventually fell into a restless sleep.

We never went to the local police department to find out what had happened to our tormented visitor. In retrospect, we should have, but it got lost in the flow of everyday living.

We never saw the girl again or had anything else like that happen during the rest of our time in that house. But I have replayed that night in my head many times over the years, and I am convinced that we made all the right choices.

As much as I wanted to save this woman from harm, my first obligation was to the two boys fast asleep upstairs in their bedrooms. I was prepared to react if and when the woman's boyfriend had shown up, but until then, she was safe and we were safe, courtesy of a heavy wooden door and a loaded gun.

We also did the right thing by calling the police. That should *always* be your first action, assuming time permits it. At a minimum, you can set down the phone, leaving the line open in order to make certain the 911 operator is a witness to the events that ensue *and* to the fact that you are not the aggressor. Such testimony could be of value in the event that you kill or injure your intruder.

And, this particular scenario, involving a boyfriend and girlfriend, had the added weight of being a domestic violence situation. As any cop will tell you, a "DV" is a strange animal—and subject to extreme volatility. It's not unusual for a woman to call 911 because her husband or boyfriend is being abusive—but when law enforcement arrives and attempts to arrest or subdue the male, the woman suddenly begins defending him, sometimes with physical force.

You always want to minimize your exposure to those situations, unless you are absolutely positive you know the lay of the land, and even then, you proceed with extreme caution. Despite my hyperaware state, I had noted the change in tone from my damsel in distress when I told her I would shoot her boyfriend. Was she a potential robber who was deflated at the thought of a loaded gun so nearby? Or was she really a troubled woman escaping a drunk or violent suitor? I'll never know for certain, but what I learned to my satisfaction that night is that I am able to overcome the intense physiological reaction to stress well enough to think clearly and make good choices. If you plan to own a gun, both are essential—and there is no way to practice that. Fortunately, I was competent enough with my gun to keep it pointed in a safe direction and to keep my finger off the trigger at all times. Only *after* I settled down did I look at the grooves in my hand and realize that I had been holding the gun so tightly that the grip checkering had left an imprint on my palm! That same pressure could have easily been transferred to my trigger finger, creating the potential for disaster, had I not been careful to follow proper form and the rules of safe gun handling.

If I was still harboring any lingering doubts about gun ownership and my ability to use my gun intelligently, that eventful night helped ease my concerns.

But it also reminded me that simply owning a gun or having a concealed carry license does *not* give you the authority to become a vigilante or to pursue truth, justice, and the American way for those in peril.

Had I ventured onto my porch with the gun or, worse yet, had I followed the woman out to the street in pursuit of her angry beau, I would have been very much in violation of the laws of the state of Ohio. Which raises another important point: know the laws of your state with regard to gun ownership, concealed carry, and personal defense. Ohio happens to be a "duty to retreat" state. That is, if you can get away from danger, you are obligated to do so. Confrontation should be a last resort. This differs from a state such as Florida, which became famous for its "stand your ground" laws, permitting you to stand and defend yourself, even if you have access to an escape route.

Each state has its own approach to personal defense and gun laws. Some, such as California and New York, take a dim view of gun ownership and will put you through endless hoops to even own a gun, let alone what you might endure if you actually have to use it. For other states, such as Georgia and Texas, gun ownership is as common as owning an automobile.

Recently, I read a note from a friend who had moved to a small town in Texas. She remarked on how unnerving it was to see people walking around town with exposed firearms. I smiled. I didn't have the heart to tell her that Ohio is also an "open carry" state, although few choose to exercise

Gun Girl Tip #5

No matter how prepared you are, no matter how much you train, you will never be 100 percent ready for a personal defense encounter. The best you can do is understand what will happen in your body—muscle tremors, tunnel vision, impaired hearing, nausea, you name it. Even seasoned police officers and combat veterans will tell you that the physical reaction to fear can never be completely overcome. Your best course of action is to become familiar enough with your gun and with your safety plan that certain actions and reactions become instinctive.

that right. There is just too much potential that an exposed firearm will induce panic within the well-intentioned but often skittish populace, so most Ohioans go the concealed carry route just to be on the safe side. Apparently Texans don't worry too much about what their "ungunned" neighbors think, or maybe most Texans are just armed to begin with. I knew I liked Texas for a reason.

CHAPTER SUMMARY

- Don't buy a gun for protection until and unless you have accepted the reality that you may have to shoot another human being.

- Owning a gun *never* authorizes/empowers you to intervene in conflict. Pulling out a weapon should always be your last resort.

- Always call 911, even if you think you will need to defend yourself prior to the arrival of the police. Leave the line open so you have a witness.

- Know the gun and personal defense laws in your state.

CHAPTER 3

WHAT NEW SHOOTERS DON'T KNOW— AND CAN'T LEARN BY WATCHING TV

Okay, yes—there are a lot of things new shooters don't understand about firearms and the mechanics of shooting. But this chapter tackles a few of the basics that some instructors either don't bother with or don't realize their students don't know!

I have a surprising number of students in my four-hour Introduction to Handguns class who have previously sat through Ohio's mandatory twelve hours of basic pistol training (which was recently lowered to eight hours) and have received their concealed carry permit. Yet they remain uneasy about carrying and woefully unfamiliar with the basics of gun handling. In most cases, I attribute this to the sheer mass of information and material that is thrown at a student during Ohio's Concealed Handgun License (CHL) training. But I also know that firearms instructors, as with every other profession, vary broadly in skill and knowledge. As a student, you should never hesitate to demand thoroughness and clarity from anyone who has taken your money in exchange for education. If you feel that you have not received thorough enough explanations, and especially if the entire class feels this way, it is incumbent on the students to set the bar higher. If the instructor does not respond, report him or her to the state attorney general's office. Most states take very seriously the proper fulfillment of concealed carry laws and licensing. I am aware of multiple cases in the state of Ohio where instructors have been prosecuted for providing incomplete training.

In most cases, however, you walk away from your class having heard much of what you need to know to safely use and carry a gun. What you may have retained, however, is an entirely different story. The state and your CHL (or CCW) instructor may have certified that you have the answers, but you are still not sure. As someone who was "gun-stupid" for much of her life, I still recall that awkward state of knowing and not knowing—and the embarrassment of wanting to ask questions that I should probably already know the answers to. As an instructor, I try to remember that *telling* my students isn't enough; I have to *show* them, and as often as possible.

I also learned early that you can't assume that beginners understand even the most basic principles of handgun usage. I didn't. Why in the world would I expect that someone else would? My foundation of firearms knowledge came from television and Hollywood, and, while today's crime shows are far more realistic than the days of *Adam-12*, *Streets of San Francisco*, or *Charlie's Angels*, there is still an inability—or unwillingness—to accurately present firearms.

So what are those things that you don't know you don't know—and you won't learn by flipping on the television?

Spending some time on a real shooting range—even if you're not shooting—will help you acquire an accurate concept of how guns react when fired. Watching TV crime shows will not. (But I still love *NCIS*.) *viicha/Shutterstock*

1. Guns jump. Some hop, others buck, and a few leap—but all guns move in your hand no matter how tightly you hold them. Why? Because you are holding a relatively small piece of equipment that has a controlled explosion taking place inside. Every time you pull that trigger, your gun goes through a complex mechanical gyration (explained in chapter 7) that results in a bullet racing the length of the barrel and bursting out of the muzzle at a tremendous rate of speed. When the bullet breaks free of the gun, the force of that action creates a flip of the muzzle as well as a backward thrust known as recoil. A small, lightweight round, such as a .22 LR, generates very manageable recoil and muzzle flip (how much the nose of the gun flips up when you fire it). A high-energy round, such as a .40 S&W, can really smack your hand, and you have to be ready for it.

Recoil and muzzle flip are determined by two factors: (a) the size and energy of the ammunition and (b) the size of the gun. A round of ammunition that is topped by a small bullet (such as .22 LR) usually produces a lesser amount of recoil and muzzle flip, relative to the size of the gun. And a large gun absorbs more recoil and is more comfortable to shoot than a small gun.

Other factors come into play, including the construction of the gun (steel framed versus polymer framed) and the design of the internal recoil spring, but, as a rule, if you want to know how much a gun will kick, compare the size of the ammunition it is chambered for versus the size and weight of the gun itself.

So, as I touched on in chapter 1, a large gun chambered for .22 LR will have barely noticeable recoil and muzzle flip—for example, target pistols, which require pinpoint accuracy, are usually larger and heavier guns with longer barrels and are chambered for .22 LR. And a small gun, perhaps a concealable 1911 with a three-inch barrel chambered for .45 ACP, will have a significant amount of recoil and muzzle flip.

Clear as mud? Probably so, especially if you are used to watching Ziva on *NCIS* take in a little target practice with her Sig Sauer .40 S&W, which, amazingly, stays perfectly level every time she fires it.

Once you become a dedicated shooter, you will find yourself getting irritated at your favorite TV crime shows, especially those that work hard to provide precise forensic detail on exactly how a bullet travels through human flesh but still can't manage to convey an accurate representation of muzzle flip. (Insert frustrated sigh.)

The author, at left, watches as a student practices aiming with a .45 ACP 1911. *Layne English*

2. All triggers are not created equal. A new shooter may not realize that every gun has a different type of trigger pull, ranging from a heavy, long pull to a "barely breathe on it" light pull. If you try a particular model and can hardly depress the trigger, fear not. There is a gun out there that is much easier to manage.

Remember my earlier analogy that guns are like shoes—you will always be able to find one that "fits." In chapter 6, we'll get more detailed about the different types of trigger pulls and what they mean. For now, just remember that the strength needed to pull a trigger can vary dramatically from gun to gun. I recall eagerly toting a Ruger Alaskan chambered for .454 Casull out to the range. The .454 is a powerful round, and I wanted to be able to tell my gun shop customers that I had fired it. I arranged my stance, acquired my sight picture, placed the pad of my index finger on the trigger, and pulled . . . and pulled . . . and pulled. Now, I am fairly petite, with skinny fingers and probably not the greatest hand strength. But this was the first time I had ever found a gun whose trigger I couldn't even budge. I finally extracted my left index finger from around the grip and laid it atop my right. Pressing with both fingers, I eventually managed to discharge the gun. I shot it four times and then gave up. The force of the recoil was considerable, but not overwhelming. The trigger pull, however, would have prevented me from ever using the gun effectively. Scratch that one off the list.

3. **If you ever (God forbid) have to shoot someone, please don't expect them to go flying backwards into the nearest wall.** It doesn't work that way. Newtonian physics comes into play: for every action there is an equal and opposite reaction. If a bullet had the kinetic energy to lift a person off their feet and propel them backward (a la Hollywood), it would have *the exact same effect* on the shooter!

It is important to have realistic expectations regarding what your gun can and can't do, lest you be surprised at the worst possible moment!

4. **That little red dot on the target means *nothing*!** I finally gave up having my introductory class students shoot at a traditional scoring target with a tiny red bull's-eye in the middle. I watched them work themselves into a frenzy and develop an advanced case of "scarlet fever" as they obsessed about hitting (not just hitting, but destroying) that red dot. If they didn't eat the dot completely out of the center, they felt they'd failed. No amount of praise or explanation on my part could modify that target fixation. So I switched the game and began providing *only* zombie targets to my students. It changed everything, and it taught the lesson I had tried and failed to teach with traditional targets: in a personal defense situation, you are *not* looking for a red dot on your intruder's body—you are shooting for body mass. *Body* mass. Body *mass*. Got it? Your ability to survive an attack by a bad guy has nothing to do with scoring. It has to do with filling his torso with bullets until he stops and/or retreats (which will happen as you begin to impact

Gun Girl Tip #6

Here is a rule of thumb:

Small (low-caliber, small bullet) ammunition + big gun = very little recoil

Small ammunition + small gun = a little more recoil

Big (high-caliber, heavy bullet) ammunition + big gun = much more recoil

Big ammunition + small gun = the most recoil

The construction of a gun impacts the comfort level of shooting and carrying it. A steel-framed gun like the Sig Sauer P238, pictured at left, is often more comfortable to shoot than a polymer-framed gun of the same caliber. In the case of the Glock 42, pictured at right, however, the two guns—both .380s—are equally comfortable to shoot.

his blood-bearing organs). Interestingly, students who had shot miserably when confronted with a red-dot target were veritable deadeyes when I switched them to zombie targets. Why? Because the purpose was not to achieve some arbitrary score but, instead, to hit the evil zombie somewhere that would prevent him from advancing his maniacal plan for world domination.

The bottom line is, when shooting for self-defense, there is no score and no red dot—there is only someone left standing at the end, and that someone should be *you*. Shoot at the biggest thing you see—body mass—and shoot until it stops coming toward you. Plain. Simple. Effective.

And, by the way, no, you will *not* be able to disable the attacker by shooting him/her in the knees, arms, shoulders, or hands—unless you hit those areas accidentally. It will be tough enough to simply hit body mass, let alone slender appendages that are moving rapidly in your direction. You always shoot to kill, not to wound. Once again, if you can't make peace with that, do not buy a gun.

5. **You don't close one eye when you shoot.** Yes, we all do it sometimes—and it is fine to start off that way, but in a tactical situation, keeping both eyes open keeps you safe. I initially argued

with my law enforcement husband on this point, explaining that I suffer from astigmatism in my right eye and, as a result, *cannot* keep both eyes open. "If I open both eyes, I see multiple front sights. It's just impossible," I argued, with just a hint of whine. John patiently suggested that I focus on the front sight with my right eye open and my left eye closed. Then, once the sight is clear, slowly begin opening my left eye. "It will still be blurry at first, but you can train that eye to focus and you'll be fine," he explained. After plenty of range time—and practice in my home using an *empty* (no magazine, nothing in the chamber) gun—I am pleased to say that it is getting easier to focus with both eyes open. Still not perfect, but much better than I was—and certainly better off in any tactical situation.

Range time is essential with any gun you plan to use for self-defense, but it will never replicate the point-and-shoot action necessary in a personal defense scenario.

6. You won't aim in a personal defense situation. Guaranteed.
The careful, methodical sight picture you acquire when shooting on the range will become a happy memory if you are confronted by a real threat. "When you had to fire your gun in the line of duty, did you actually take the time to aim?" I asked my hubby. He shook his head no. "To be honest, you don't remember that much about what you do or don't do in a high-stress situation, but no, I don't recall aiming in the traditional sense. I had practiced enough with my gun that I knew what to expect, so I relied on my natural aim point and pulled the trigger."

What? Natural aim point? Did you know that you have such a thing? Well, yeah. Look at something on your wall and close your eyes. With your eyes closed, point to the item. Nine times out of ten, you will be spot on or very close—and that's with no vision at all. When you point a gun, you are, in effect, pointing an extension of your finger. In a personal defense situation, you will be operating on instinct, which is why it is so important to practice with the gun you intend to carry or keep for home defense. That instinct will allow you to shoot pretty accurately in the direction that you are pointing your finger.

And, by the way, you likely won't hold the gun exactly perfectly, nor will you stand with your feet shoulder-width apart, knees slightly bent, wrists locked, etc. No, you will be fighting for your life, and the only thing that will matter is that you point the gun and pull the trigger.

7. **Guns aren't inherently evil, and owning a gun—and learning to use it safely and competently—doesn't make you unfeminine or a bad mom.** Yep, I have actually had women ask me how I reconciled being a firearms instructor (and gun salesperson) with being a mom. To me, there is no disconnect; in fact, the two roles go hand in hand. Nothing is more important to me than my son and his well-being. Popular media do a pretty good job of presenting a plethora of doting mothers, and, in recent years, they have even managed to present some strong women who love guns—Ziva in *NCIS* and Fiona in *Burn Notice* spring to mind. But I cannot recall seeing any doting mothers who love guns! Apparently, the two don't mix in TV land, but, I can assure you, they go together quite nicely in real life.

Although I may have started life as a "fighting young liberal," the pistol-packin' mama of today would willingly stand, gun in hand, between harm and my son or husband or any other member of my family who was being threatened. To me, that is the very essence of my "femininity"—a bald-faced conviction to protect those I love and to quickly dispatch anyone who threatens them. And no, I would not worry about my gun being taken away from me and used against me because I would not allow the intruder to get that close. If I pull a gun and point it at you, I intend to use it. Period.

8. **Lasers are a nice tool, but they are *not* a deterrent.** There is a popular myth that is perpetuated in gun counter discussions across the fruited plain—usually by the people with the least amount of experience—that pointing a thin red (or green) laser at someone's chest will dissuade them from any mischief they might be intent on committing. Just the other day at the gun counter, I heard it again: "Yeah, when they see that little ol' red dot come to rest over

The number of female shooters and instructors has exploded over the past decade. Women aren't just buying guns, but they are also actively and enthusiastically participating in the shooting lifestyle.

their heart, they'll be outta there in a flash," says the "old pro" counter king who is usually trying to impress some newbie next to him. (Explanation: Every gun shop has its "counter kings," my term for those folks who come in weekly, if not daily, to visit, chat, scope out the new guns, and lend their wisdom—or sometimes lack thereof—to the proceedings. When I was flying, I learned that the term "hangar queen" referred both to an airplane that spent more time in the hangar for maintenance than in the air and to those folks who wandered in and sat around for much of the day, swapping tales and offering advice but never actually getting into the cockpit. I quickly discovered that airplanes and firearms share an abundance of tale tellers and shop sitters.)

When I hear these laser debates at the gun counter (as I have heard many times), I look to my law enforcement co-workers, who are usually shaking their heads in disbelief. They are quick to point out a number of reasons why you should *never* rely on a laser to prevent you from having to pull the trigger: (a) A laser does *not* help you see the target more clearly—it is a thin red stream of light, not a bright flare—plus, in a darkened room, even if it helps you focus on the target, it also makes it much easier for the target to follow that red line right back to where *you* are standing. (b) A laser can easily show your intruder just how nervous you are. Lasers shake, even in the calmest of hands, but if you are scared—and you will be if you're pointing that laser at an intruder—then the modest vibration of that light beam quickly becomes a pulsating spasm. (c) Depending on the

Take the time on the range with a competent instructor to learn how to shoot accurately; don't depend on a laser to do it for you.

model of laser, it can take more than a second or two to get it activated. And, while you are struggling to turn on your laser, the intruder has just closed the distance between the two of you and is deftly relieving you of your weapon. There are several popular personal defense guns with built-in lasers that are just plain frustrating to activate. It requires heavy finger pressure and an awkward hand movement to turn on the laser. In a high-stress situation, with the loss of fine motor skills, you will be hard-pressed to press hard enough to activate the laser! I tell my students and customers that I would much rather they be directing their energy toward pointing and shooting, versus trying to turn on a laser that has little defensive value.

All that having been said, there are those who will argue passionately in favor of lasers. I cannot tell you they aren't useful in certain situations—I can only tell you that they should never take the place of pulling the trigger.

CHAPTER SUMMARY

● Enjoy your television crime shows, but don't expect that anything you see on them will accurately depict real-life gun usage. There may be a few exceptions, but make sure you know how your gun will really respond, not how it appears to respond on *CSI*, *NCIS*, or *Criminal Minds*.

● If you try a particular model and you don't like how it feels in your hands, how heavy the trigger pulls, or how violently it recoils, don't give up on guns. There is something out there that will fit your hands, strength, and wallet. I guarantee it.

● Using a gun doesn't make you less of a woman (or more of a man). Done right, it makes you less of a victim and a more safe, secure, and competent shooter.

● A laser is a tool not a deterrent; if you are attacked, it is far more important to pull the trigger than to activate the laser.

CHAPTER 4

THE BASICS OF SAFETY

Early in my "gun career," I figured out there was a lot I didn't know. My friend Mike had worked with me on shooting stance and the basics of safe gun handling, and had even gifted me with an NRA Basic Pistol class for Christmas.

The twelve-hour class (which has since been shortened to eight by the state) was informative and fun, and, in Ohio, it gave me the legal authority to apply for my concealed carry permit, which I did with glee. But, even though the state deemed me fit to carry a gun, I knew that my rudimentary knowledge from one day in the classroom was not enough to make me competent. I wanted more.

I began training to be an instructor and a range officer and signed up for any other NRA class I could afford to take. They were fun and informative, but I still felt that something was missing. I needed to immerse myself in firearms, not only to become a safe user but a skilled instructor, as well.

At Mike's urging, I drafted a letter to a local gun shop. I had been familiar with Olde English Outfitters for years. Formerly known as Olde English Gun Shoppe, the place is a virtual firearms mecca in the West Central Ohio region. My ex-hubby and I had visited the shop many times, picking up long guns for local Ducks Unlimited or other conservation group auctions and raffles.

Started in 1974 by Ron English, Olde English Outfitters has a reputation for integrity, customer service, and gun knowledge up the wazoo. Ron had long since turned the business over to his son Evan, and I knew Evan to be a good businessman, a firearms expert, and a fair and wise leader.

With a knot in my stomach, I drafted a letter to Evan that said, in part, "I don't pretend to have a great deal of gun knowledge. That's really

Gun Girl Tip #7

If you question the value of hunters, take some time to follow the money. The US Fish and Wildlife Service reports that "each year, nearly $200 million in hunters' federal excise taxes are distributed to state agencies to support wildlife management programs, the purchase of lands open to hunters, and hunter education and safety classes. Proceeds from the Federal Duck Stamp, a required purchase for migratory waterfowl hunters, have purchased more than five million acres of habitat for the refuge system" as of 2005. And those figures don't even count the massive infusions of funding, habitat, and awareness generated by organizations such as Ducks Unlimited, Pheasants Forever, the National Wild Turkey Federation, and others. The International Hunter Education Association points out that "hunters do more to help wildlife than any other group in America," pouring almost $400 million per year into conservation. So much for my early impression of hunters as drunken, gun-crazed rednecks. I would come to believe that hunters understand and respect firearms, the sanctity of life, and man's stewardship of this earth better than just about anyone else.

why I would love to work there, so I can grow in my knowledge and skill." I quickly added that I understood he could not run a business by hiring people who knew nothing about his industry, but that I would "happily sweep floors, stock shelves, or do whatever is needed around the shop just to get the chance to learn more about firearms." I pledged, "I will work hard and make myself an asset to your organization in exchange for this opportunity."

I was not proud; I would have accepted any role in the shop just to get that chance to learn more. It is an approach I took thirty years ago as a fledgling in the newspaper industry and, later on, when I was learning to fly an airplane: put yourself around people who know the business inside and out, soak up their knowledge, ask all the "dumb questions" (and you'll usually find out the questions aren't so dumb, after all), and, most of all, shut up and pay attention.

To my shock and pleasure, Evan contacted me after several weeks. He told me he thought I had potential and asked me to report to work on an April morning. I showed up ready to sweep, stack, or sort—and found myself in training behind the gun counter.

I panicked.

"Uh, Evan, you know I am pretty new to all this. I mean, I've taken classes to become an instructor, but I still feel really inadequate when it comes to overall knowledge of firearms, especially specific models," I said tentatively.

Evan smiled and nodded, "You know that you *don't* know—and that's a step in the right direction. I know you'll be in there asking questions, taking guns apart to see how they work, and soaking up all the knowledge you can. I also think you'll be a good fit with the gun counter crew. That's important. Just pay attention. Use the knowledge you have, and build on it. You'll learn."

Gun Girl Tip #8

Sometimes, leaving your comfort zone is the quickest way to expand your knowledge. Don't be afraid to ask for help—and to push yourself a little past the place where you feel most at home.

To this day, I marvel at his wisdom in dropping me right into the thick of things. I didn't want to disappoint him, and I wanted to earn the respect of my all-male, mostly retired cop coworkers on the gun counter.

It was arguably the best professional decision I have ever made. But the knowledge did not come easily or overnight. It took effort on my part, and that effort began with the barest of basics, so that's exactly where I begin with any new shooters.

My first day on the job consisted of shadowing one of the managers and listening intently as he sold guns, explained the advantages of specific models, and responded thoughtfully to customer questions.

I was fortunate to find my way into a gun shop that stressed customer service above all else. As a consumer, I had been in far too many shops where I was completely ignored, perhaps because I was female—or maybe the shop's owner just didn't have Evan's sense of urgency about customer service.

Either way, I had learned early that there were definitely jerks to be found behind gun counters. But Evan encouraged and, in fact, demanded a different approach. Maybe because of his faith-based perspective on life or perhaps because he had a business degree, he urged us to take time with customers and walk them through the pros and cons of their choices. And, thus, I ended up being the "go-to gal" for new shooters and, particularly, new female shooters. I am not sure it was intentional, but the ladies seemed to gravitate in my direction, and, after a few months, my male counterparts would often direct a novice lady shooter toward me, saying, "Tara can give you the best perspective on what might work for you." It made me proud (and sometimes a little nervous).

I vividly remember my first sale—to a lady who had never shot before and wasn't certain if she ever intended to carry. "I want something that'll be comfortable to shoot and that will at least work as a home defense gun," she explained. "I might want to carry it but I'm really not sure. I've held some guns at other shops . . . revolvers mostly, but they just don't feel good in my hand and I'm not sure what the recoil will be like."

She had a long list of questions for me, explaining that she had made the same inquiries at other gun shops, only to be dismissed or mollified with a canned answer.

"So, I am going to ask *you* these questions," she said hopefully. "First, what's the most important thing I need to know about owning a gun?"

That one was easy.

"Never point it at anything you don't intend to shoot," I said quickly. "But it goes beyond that. Safety is essential if you plan to own a gun. Nothing I tell you today is as important as that emphasis on safety."

Gun Girl Tip #9

Find a gun shop that caters to and cares about what female customers want. And that *isn't* necessarily the dude who carries all the ladies' T-shirts, bra holsters, and lacy shooting bustiers. It may be the gruff old codger who treats everyone with respect and doesn't care if you are male, female, black, white, gay, straight, or from Jupiter—he only wants to make you *safe*. There are plenty of good gun stores out there; don't settle for one that doesn't want your business.

It's the same message I share with my students over and over again— and then over again, usually when they are so ready to move on to something else.

The NRA identifies three primary rules of safe gun handling:

1. Always keep the muzzle of the gun pointed in a safe direction.

2. Always keep your finger extended along the frame until you are ready to shoot.

3. Always keep the gun unloaded until you are ready to shoot.

I have a few more to add to this list, but let's start by explaining the first three.

1. Always keep the muzzle of the gun pointed in a safe direction.

Number 1 means *exactly* what it says: the muzzle of your gun (the business end where the bullets come out) should be kept away from anything you don't intend to shoot.

But what *is* a safe direction? Well, on a range it is usually keeping the gun pointed at a forty-five-degree angle toward the ground or pointed toward the targets downrange in the "low ready position." If you are indoors, then keep it pointed at the ground and away from any living thing. I can't stress this one enough. If you never follow any rule but this one, you will likely stay safe, because that gun will never have the opportunity to discharge when it is pointed at something precious.

Now, some folks will tell you that "safe" is keeping the barrel pointed upward. Certainly, that is preferable to pointing it at a person, but it is *not* an optimal direction. You often see video footage of celebratory folks in the Middle East firing their guns into the air—but what you *don't* see is those bullets returning to earth at terminal velocity. If you happen to be standing beneath one when it comes down, it will likely hurt you and could even kill you.

For a little verification on this, I dug into *Hatcher's Notebook*, a treasure trove of ballistics and gunsmithing data published in the late 1950s by Julian Hatcher, the former NRA director and technical editor of *American Rifleman* magazine.

While much of the book contains formulas and tables that make my eyes cross and my brain melt, there are still some fascinating discussions about the fallacy of exploding bullets (something my students often worry about) and the impact of air and gravity on a moving bullet.

When you are on the firing line but not shooting, you can hold your gun in the low ready position, pointed down range toward the targets, until it's your time to shoot.

Hatcher performed a number of experiments on the potential damage done by a falling bullet. He determined that a .30-caliber rifle round would fall to earth at a rate of three hundred feet per second. That sounds like a lot, until you consider that it comes out of the muzzle at about 2,700 feet per second. Obviously, it is not nearly as dangerous falling to earth as it is exiting the muzzle. But, one source compared the blow from a falling bullet to being hit in the head with a hammer or a two-by-four board. I don't know about you folks, but neither of those scenarios appeal to me. And, yes, either one could potentially kill you.

I wandered off onto this rabbit trail mainly because there are numerous online debates about the potential lethality of falling bullets. The bottom line is that firing a gun straight into the air is not a safe action for any number of reasons, only one of which is that gravity might come back and bite you on the rear.

Another reason not to fire upward is one my husband, John, learned the hard way when he was a young sheriff's deputy and competitive shooter.

"It was pretty embarrassing at the time," he explained. "That is, *after* I regained my hearing, realized I hadn't shot myself, and had made certain that I hadn't killed my next-door neighbor."

Alone one evening in his bachelor trailer, John decided to clean his competition gun and several other pistols in his possession, including his father's service revolver.

"I turned on the TV, laid out my cleaning kit and my pistols, and started working on my competition gun. At some point in the process, I set down my gun briefly and then picked it back up to begin checking the timing," he related, explaining that competitive shooters check the timing by listening carefully as the internal machinery engages when the trigger is pulled. "I was making sure the bolt locked in before the hammer fell."

Unfortunately, my professionally trained, highly skilled hubby (who was still a little wet behind the ears way back then) picked up the wrong gun. He hoisted his father's service revolver and held it inches from his right ear. Pulling the trigger released the hammer right into the primer cup of a .357 Magnum round, which exploded from the muzzle and knocked John backwards (and out, he believes) before exiting the trailer via a window.

"I learned a lot of lessons that night," he says, shaking his head. "Chief among them is 'safety first'—always check the chamber on any gun you pick up! I also discovered that there's a reason why you don't point a gun into the air and fire it, especially if you aren't wearing ear protection. It took days for my hearing to return to normal. Likewise, the old rule of 'keep the muzzle pointed in a safe direction' took on a brand new reality as I examined the direction the bullet had exited the window and realized, with a cold chill, that it could very well have traveled into the trailer next door."

To this day, John remembers his panicked race next door, expecting to find a mortally wounded neighbor. Thankfully, the bullet had first blasted through the carport, which had not only redirected it but also slowed it down. The neighbor was fine. John was understandably rattled but grateful to be neither killer nor victim.

"It also bothered me how close I came to shooting myself that night. And if I'd succeeded, everyone would have assumed I was a suicide victim, especially since I was a professional and—in theory anyway—shouldn't have been making such stupid mistakes," he says.

But stupid mistakes happen to *everyone*, and, most of my cop friends tell me that the more comfortable you are with firearms, the more potential you have to get careless.

My husband's story underscores several vital safety warnings: (a) Firing a gun near your ear isn't smart. Period. (b) Keeping that muzzle pointed in a

Most ranges require that you keep your gun pointed downward at a forty-five-degree angle when you are not shooting. This way an unintentional shot hits the ground, not a fellow shooter or your own foot.

safe direction isn't something you do simply when you are on the range. You do it when you are driving, sitting, cleaning, and, yes, checking the timing on an "empty" gun. (c) You should *never* have live ammunition nearby when cleaning a gun. And, finally, John's story illustrates one of my standard rules for safe gun handling (discussed below): assume every gun you pick up is loaded.

And please remember that what appears to be a safe direction may, in fact, not be so safe. If you are in your home or any building, there is a temptation to turn the muzzle toward a wall. But, modern construction being what it is, that may not be a good idea, especially if there are people on the other side of the wall. Standard ball-tip range rounds can penetrate drywall, and their velocity is not significantly impacted while passing through it. So an inadvertent shot of your 9mm or .45 or .357 through a modern construction wall has the potential to seriously injure, perhaps even kill, someone standing on the other side. Keeping that muzzle pointed in a safe direction isn't always as easy as it sounds.

2. Always keep your finger off the trigger until you are ready to shoot.

I have a dear friend—we'll call him Buddy—whose passion for firearms knows no bounds. He is especially enamored of European guns and can tell you more about Mausers and Mosin-Nagants than you could possibly

Keeping your trigger finger extended along the frame is essential to safe gun handling.

ever want to hear. But my friend has a perplexing problem when it comes to keeping his finger off the trigger. The poor man simply can't hold a gun for ten seconds before that index finger drifts onto the trigger. I've seen him do it in classes, I've seen him do it on the range, and I've seen him do it when shopping for firearms at the gun counter. He is aware of his tendency and even grins sheepishly when trainers threaten to splint his finger to the frame.

Gun Girl Tip #10

Your instructor may bark at you to "index your finger!" That's a quick way of saying "get your freakin' finger off the freakin' trigger!" I simply shout "Finger! Finger! Finger!" if the situation is too immediate for lengthy explanation.

But, on one particular occasion, his wandering finger almost caused a tragedy.

During a visit with several friends one afternoon, Buddy pulled out his newest acquisition—a small, portable .380—and proceeded to show it off to the gents seated in his living room. Now, Buddy isn't stupid—as a trained instructor, he knew he needed to clear the weapon before handing it to his friends. Buddy grabbed the slide of the gun with his fleshy hand and yanked it backwards. And, typical of the small, concealable .380s, such as the Ruger LCP and the Kel-Tec P-3AT, the slide was awkward to grip and Buddy lost his hold on it. The slide leapt forward, and, as it did, the firearm discharged, sending a bullet ricocheting off the tile floor, narrowly missing the family dog and coming to rest in the dining room.

When Buddy relayed the story several days later, those of us who know and love him nodded in unison, absolutely certain that the gun discharged because Buddy's finger was where it always is—squarely on that trigger. But Buddy was in denial. To this day, he insists that he has no idea how such a well-made little firearm could have malfunctioned like that. He went so far as to contact the manufacturer to inquire about the frequency of such phenomena. Not surprisingly, he was told that they had no reports of any such thing ever happening—unless you happened to have your finger on the trigger when the slide slapped forward.

Of course, the other aspect of this incident is that Buddy had dragged out a loaded gun to show off. That, in and of itself, is not necessarily a bad thing, but, while clearing it, he either already had a round in the chamber (again, not typically a problem) or he did not drop the magazine first. When the slide slapped forward, it moved a round into the open chamber, making it possible for the firing pin to strike the primer as he unconsciously gripped the trigger.

On the plus side, Buddy did remember the first rule of gun safety—he kept the muzzle pointed in a reasonably safe direction, thus preventing anything worse than an embarrassing moment.

3. Always keep the gun unloaded until you are ready to shoot.

This is the one I always have to explain—and the one that confused the heck out of me as a novice shooter. I tried to take it to its logical conclusion and imagined frantically loading my gun as someone battered down my door in the middle of the night!

The truth is, the NRA might have been able to develop a better wording for this safety tip, but darned if I have been able to come up with it.

Gun Girl Tip #11

The NRA and similar national gun organizations have great safety guidelines, but don't stop there. Safety isn't about slogans; it is a lifestyle and a mindset. (Hey, that's a great slogan!)

I tell my students that what it really means is "always keep the gun unloaded until you are ready to use it for its intended purpose." That's a lot wordier but hopefully it conveys the following: If you purchase a Sig Sauer P238 as a carry gun, you will load it just before you tuck it into your purse or your pocket holster. If you buy a Springfield XD as a home defense gun, you will load it just before you set it inside the gun safe next to your bed. And if you buy a Browning Buck Mark as a plinking gun (a gun that is used for fun range shooting only), you will load it once you are at the range and on the firing line.

In only one of those instances are you actually loading the gun right before you fire it. The rest of them require that the gun be loaded long before you actually hoist it up to acquire your sight picture.

My additional safety admonitions include:

4. Know what lies beyond.

My ex drummed this into my head each and every time we went hunting. "If you shoot at that deer and miss, you make damn sure you know what's on the other side of the animal. And not just within a few feet but within a couple hundred yards. Bullets can travel a long way," he warned.

When dropping the magazine to check if a gun is loaded, you will usually depress a small button located beside the trigger guard, like it is on this Kel-Tec-P3AT.

Not every magazine release is a button. On Walthers, for example, you pull down on a lever located on the trigger guard.

Some European models feature the mag release at the butt of the grip. If you don't see it anywhere else, look for it here!

I paid attention, and not just when deer hunting. I paid attention when squirrel hunting, rabbit hunting, and duck hunting. Although ducks are typically shot on the wing, it's not unusual to try to snag one as it sets its wings and drops into the blocks (a.k.a. decoys) or as it rises off the water in flight. Such events are exciting, and, if you are in a public hunting area, it is easy to forget that there are other blinds not far from yours.

I remember my ex returning from a hunt one day with mysterious red welts all over his face. They were made redder by the fact that he was furious. The guy in the blind across the bay had gotten overly excited about a large raft of birds and had fired directly toward my ex's blind. Even allowing for wind, gravity, and other factors, those pellets still found their way into the blind with enough force to break skin.

Matt had no tolerance for stupidity with a gun, and he gave the careless hunter a verbal lashing for his stupidity. But, it should be noted, Matt did *not* threaten or attempt to shoot the other gentleman. Two wrongs don't make a right.

5. Assume every gun you pick up is loaded.

And, precisely, how do you do this? One of my big embarrassments when I first learned to shoot was that, despite multiple classes and plenty of range time, I still didn't understand exactly how to clear a gun (that is, what I should do and in what order) and what, exactly, I was looking for when clearing the gun (that is, checking to make certain it was unloaded).

After one or two classes, you become hesitant to ask "dumb questions"—even if they were never adequately answered during class time.

So here are the basic steps for clearing (a.k.a. checking) a handgun to see that it is not loaded.

Before you do anything else, no matter what kind of gun you are clearing, you always point that muzzle down and away from anything living or valuable. That is the only thing that saved my pal Buddy from needing to get a new dog, new friends, or new body parts.

With a semi-automatic gun, the first thing you do is drop the magazine. Depress that little button beside the trigger guard (in the case of a Walther, pull down on the little lever at the base of the trigger guard, or, on some European guns, push back the button on the butt of the gun) and let the magazine drop.

Next, grab the slide firmly at the back with your whole hand (not just fingers), taking advantage of the serrations on either side to get a good grip. Pull

Rack the slide back using your whole hand, not just your fingers. Those serrations on either side of the slide are there for a purpose: jam your fingertips into them as you yank backward with your dominant hand and push forward with your non-dominant hand.

Peer into the chamber or breech to make sure there is not a round lodged in it.

the slide back and peek into the breech (the resulting opening that exposes the chamber). If a bullet is already chambered, it should pop out through the ejection port (that hole in the top of the slide) when you pull the slide back—but you still want to peek into the open action and make certain you don't see a gold or silver bullet casing nestled in the chamber.

Clearing a revolver is a much easier process. Assuming you are holding a standard, modern double-action revolver, all you do is press the cylinder release button forward toward the cylinder with your right hand (assuming you are right-handed) and push the cylinder toward you from the other side of the gun using your left

New students worry that they won't be able to see a live round in the chamber, but it is pretty obvious once you know what you're looking for.

hand. In some cases, you may have to depress the cylinder release button against the frame, as with a Ruger LCR, or pull it back toward you, as with most Colt revolvers. Then peek into the cylinder holes and make sure they are all empty. If you are truly anal, you can push the ejection rod so that any invisible bullets can fall free.

There. You have just cleared two guns. While every gun is different, and there are occasional deviations in the location of the magazine release button or the ease with which you can yank back the slide, this is still the basic process you will follow any time you check a gun.

And *when* should you check a gun? *Every single time you pick one up.*

When I am manning the gun counter at the gun shop with six other salesmen, we may pull the same gun out of the case fifteen times in an hour. If I see that Randy just put the Kel-Tec P-11 back in the case, it doesn't mean I can or should assume that it is unloaded. I still pull it out, rack that slide, and peer into the chamber before I hand it to a customer.

Indeed, our greatest danger behind the gun counter usually comes from customers themselves who are trading in old guns that they swear are unloaded. I vividly recall the lady who brought in an aging pistol that she had inherited from a deceased uncle. "My cousin checked it and told me it's

Gun Girl Tip #12

If you have already dropped the magazine, then the slide will *not* lock back when you pull it. A slide only locks back (a) when an empty magazine is in the gun, (b) after you have fired the last round of ammunition in the magazine, or (c) if you manually set the slide lock lever as you are pulling the slide back. To manually lock back the slide, press up on the slide lock—which is the same thing as the slide release, depending on which way you are pressing it—as you pull back on the slide.

unloaded," she announced confidently, as she swept the counter and everyone behind it while bouncing the gun nervously in her hand.

"Welllll, let's just take a look at that," said slow-talking Mike, as he gently lifted the gun from her fluttering hand. "Well, looky here . . ."

Sure enough, her cousin had either not bothered to actually check the gun or had no idea what he was looking for. Because there in the chamber was a nice, shiny bullet just waiting for one of her chubby little fingers to flutter onto the trigger.

Yikes.

6. Never attempt to use a gun if you are in an "altered" state.

Most of us (hopefully) are smart enough to leave the gun in its case when we are taking prescription pain meds or have just enjoyed a glass or two of wine. But how many of us think that a non-narcotic, over-the-counter cold remedy—or the cold itself—is a cause for caution? Well, I almost learned the hard way that an altered state can be achieved very easily—and with little awareness of the degree of alteration!

A number of years ago, I was assisting with a concealed carry class. I had been fighting a head cold for several days and had been mainlining Nyquil at night and Dayquil during daylight hours. I had spent eight hours in the classroom the day before and had managed to present my portion of the class without any real issues, other than frequent nose blowing.

But I felt annoyingly fuzzy headed as I drove to the range the next morning. Still, I assured myself that the Dayquil would quickly kick in and I would be fine. Once at the range, I assembled my shooting belt, slid the holster onto it, and began setting up targets and sorting through student certificates. I absently shoved my unloaded Springfield XD into my holster, with the intention of loading it before the students arrived.

Thankfully, I never got around to it.

To manually lock open the slide, press up on the slide lock with your thumb. To release/close the slide, press down.

I had noticed, in a somewhat detached way, that the gun did not slide into its holster quite as smoothly as normal. But the cobwebs in my head didn't register the potential for a problem, and I went merrily on my way sniffling, coughing, and sneezing through the setup period. About halfway through the session, one of the other range officers looked at me oddly and said, "Uh, what's up with your holster?" I shook my head and ran my hand over the molded plastic Blackhawk, ready to defend my choice of holsters. It was then I noticed that, somehow, I had managed to slide the holster onto my gun belt *backwards*. Worse than that, I had managed to wedge my gun into it so snugly that I could not pull it loose.

Shocked? Well, it gets worse. Consumed by embarrassment, and still not thinking clearly, I began to frantically tug on the gun, hoping to dislodge it from its almost-permanent resting place in the backwards holster. Mid-tug, I felt my blood run cold as I heard and felt a sudden, distinct "click." I had just pulled the trigger of my XD. Nearly 100 percent of the time, I wore that gun loaded when on the range. It's just a smart thing to do when you are dealing with an assemblage of strangers who are all carrying loaded weapons. Had I been cognizant enough to do so on that day, I would have most certainly shot myself in the foot—or worse, based on how much I was twisting and struggling with the holster.

Rattled and miserable, I finally pulled the gun free from the holster and excused myself to go sit in my car and ponder my stupidity. It scared the crap out of me—and it gave me an awareness of just how much the haze of a head

Once you have freed the cylinder on your revolver by pressing the cylinder release button, push the cylinder out using the fingers of your non-dominant hand.

Press down on the ejection rod to clear any stubborn casings from the chambers.

cold and the cumulative effect of the meds I was taking conspired to dim my capacity to think.

I don't tell this story proudly, but if I am going to share the cautionary tales from friends and family, I need to be honest about my own screw-ups. And this was a biggie.

I have since made it a point to minimize any chance that I am teaching or shooting on days when I am sick or medicated (even with nondrowsy formulas).

Granted, you don't always have that option—but it is critical to understand that the cautions about being "under the influence" apply to a variety of altered states. Even emotional turmoil can scramble your ability to think and shoot straight.

Are you beginning to see why the need for safety is so urgent around firearms? It isn't that these tools are inherently dangerous. Modern guns and ammunition are very well made and quite dependable when used *as they are intended to be used*. It is *people* who are somewhat less predictable. And, thus, you must always be vigilant lest the people around you malfunction and create a problem with firearms.

Guns don't cause accidents any more than cars do. Stupidity, carelessness, and ignorance— all people induced—cause firearms accidents.

Fortunately, most of these conditions are curable with practice, determination, and a never-ending commitment to safety.

So those are the basics of safe gun handling. I gave a similar explanation to my very first gun customer, and I have continued to drive home those essentials in class after class and sale after sale over the years. I don't think I went into quite this much detail with my first-ever gun customer, but I probably came close, since the guys teased me about whether I'd been invited to Christmas dinner or had become a potential adoptee.

And, unknown to me, my boss, Evan, had been standing in the office around the corner. As my first-ever customer trotted happily toward the cash register to pay for a brand new Walther PK380, Evan peeked around the corner, and, in his typical "man of few words" fashion, nodded crisply and said, "Nice job. Very nice job."

I beamed with pride and headed off in search of a new customer.

CHAPTER SUMMARY

* Make it your business to learn everything you can about guns and shooting *before* you commit to becoming a gun owner.

* You will never be so skilled with a gun that you can disregard the basic safety rules. In fact, the more comfortable you are with firearms, the more vigilant you must be about observing the safety rules.

* Seek out those with knowledge and experience—and pay attention!

* A "safe direction" is downrange or pointed at the ground.

* Practice keeping your finger off the trigger (try carrying an empty gun around the house until it feels comfortable).

* Never use a gun when you are in an altered state—which includes not only drugs or alcohol, but sleeplessness, a head cold, and even over-the-counter medications.

CHAPTER 5

PIECES AND PARTS— A TOUR OF YOUR GUN

Identifying your gun piece by piece may sound ridiculously basic, but I learned early in my gun counter career that new shooters get lost in terminology. At least that's how I felt. Even after I became an instructor, there were plenty of questions rolling around in my head. The internet was helpful but by no means perfect. Being married to a lawman-turned-gun-shop-manager certainly gave me a leg up, but, even then, I often hesitated to display my ignorance to my new hubby. Lord knows he would see it in its glory often enough!

So I silently struggled with the multiple terms I heard bandied about the gun counter—What's the difference between a magazine and a clip? Where does a barrel start and a bore or muzzle end? What's the difference between the breech and the chamber? And on and on.

So this chapter is for all of you with "stupid questions" about how your gun works.

REVOLVERS

Let's start with a revolver, sometimes called a wheel gun. Why? Because the cylinder spins like a wheel. The cylinder looks like the photo at right.

It has five, six, or more holes (or chambers) in it, into which you place the ammunition (with the ball tip or front of the bullet—the rounded end—

The cylinder of a revolver spins either clockwise or counterclockwise, thus the nickname "wheel gun."

facing the front, or muzzle, of the gun). On a double-action revolver, the cylinder is attached to a crane, which swings out for ease of loading and unloading. On a single-action revolver, the cylinder can actually be removed completely from the frame by sliding out a rod positioned beneath the barrel. Single-action revolvers also have a loading gate, which allows you drop in rounds one hole at a time, without dislodging the cylinder. But on most modern double-action revolvers, you will swing out the cylinder to load it, then push it back into the frame (rotating it slightly to make sure it locks into place).

And, in case you are thinking "double-action, single-action—what the heck does that mean?" don't worry; we'll get to that in chapter 6. But let's stick with the parts for now.

Gun Girl Tip #13

No, your questions are not stupid. Stupid is assuming you know how any gun works and *not* asking the questions.

The crane allows the cylinder to swing out for ease of loading, unloading, and cleaning.

Muzzle
Front Sight
Slide
Back Sight
Trigger
Mag Release
Front Strap
Grip Panel
Magazine
Back Strap

Barrel
Cylinder
Hammer
Cylinder Release
Trigger Guard
Beavertail
Grip

Semi-automatics and revolvers share many common parts but are also very different in their operation.

A single-action revolver features a loading gate which, if you flip it open, allows you to load one round at a time into the cylinder.

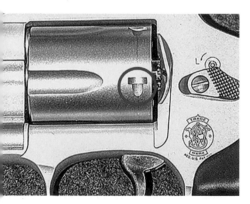

The locking notches on the cylinder look like little arrowheads. The direction they point is the direction the cylinder will spin.

Each time you pull the trigger, the cylinder rotates one chamber over (either left or right), lining up a fresh round with the barrel/bore. If you want to know which way the cylinder will rotate, look at the locking notches at the back edge of cylinder—they look like little arrowheads. The tip of the arrowhead will point in the direction that the cylinder moves.

The bore is the interior of the barrel through which the bullet travels before exiting the muzzle. The bore is "rifled" with ridges and grooves (usually called lands and grooves) that are etched in a twisting pattern, causing the bullet to spin as it races the length of the barrel.

And why the spinning? Well, if you've ever thrown a football, you'll understand. Toss a football straight toward someone and it will flop awkwardly end over end and probably thud to the ground far short of your target. But put a little spin on that hummer and just watch the accuracy and distance you get.

In technical terms, those lands and grooves serve to "gyroscopically stabilize the bullet and improve its aerodynamics"—that is, how well and how far it flies. You'll often hear gun people discussing the "twist rate" on the rifling. If you look up twist rate online, you will find a mind-numbing selection of mathematical formulas and explanations. You are welcome to return to those definitions and explore them until your head explodes. But, for now, I will give you my law enforcement hubby's simple explanations of twist rate: "Twist rate gives you two numbers, for example 1:6. The first number represents one complete revolution of the bullet within the bore, and the second number is the number of inches required for one complete spin, based on the design

A typical trigger and trigger guard on a standard concealed carry revolver.

of the lands and grooves. If you have a 1:6 twist rate and your gun has a six-inch barrel, then you know that the bullet spins one full revolution before exiting the barrel. If you have a nine-inch barrel with that same twist rate, it spins one and a half times."

So now we know that the bullet is dropped, business end first, into one of the chambers in the cylinder and that rifling makes it spin as it travels down the bore (the interior of the barrel) and out the muzzle. Of course, in order for this sequence to take place, the cylinder must be attached to something, the frame of the gun. The frame is simply the part that everything else hangs off of. Consider it your gun's torso.

Hanging off the bottom of the frame is the trigger guard and trigger. Together they look like the photo above.

The trigger is the piece you pull in order to fire the gun. This is true on almost every model ever made. I say "almost" because there have been some wacky guns created, and I never assume I've seen them all.

The trigger is attached to the internal "trigger group." The trigger group includes all parts of the gun that initiate the firing of the bullet. This includes the trigger itself, which is normally a lever that you depress with the index finger of your dominant hand; the sear, which holds the hammer back until the trigger has been pulled; and some additional interior springs.

In a traditional revolver, the function of the trigger is one of two things: (a) to release the manually cocked hammer (this is called a single-action revolver) or (b) to both cock *and* release the hammer (this is called a double-action revolver). The terms *single-action* and *double-action* refer to the work performed by the trigger and will be explained in more detail in chapter 6.

This is an older model, with the firing pin built onto the hammer.

This is a newer model, where the flat hammer strikes a transfer bar which then strikes the firing pin.

The trigger guard is the round or squared loop of flat metal or plastic that protects the trigger and prevents you from inadvertently brushing it.

Above the trigger guard, attached to the frame (the torso) of the gun, you'll see a button of some type (assuming you have a modern double-action revolver). If you press that button either forward, down, or back, depending on the model, as you push on the cylinder from the left side of the gun, your cylinder will swing out on the crane and allow you to load it.

When you pull the trigger on a revolver, a series of events takes place. First, the cylinder rotates so that a new chamber is lined up with the bore.

Internally (assuming you are using a double-action revolver), your pressure on the trigger cocks the hammer back, and the movement of the hammer compresses a metal spring in the grip (or what you might call the handle). Once the trigger is pulled completely back, it releases the now-cocked hammer, and the compressed spring drives the hammer forward. Depending on the age and model of the gun, the hammer may strike a transfer bar which then strikes a firing pin, which hits the primer cup on the ammunition and initiates a small explosion inside the cartridge. Or, the hammer claw may have a built-in firing pin that strikes the primer on the ammunition cartridge (this is usually true on older models). The photos above show the difference between a modern hammer and one of the older styles with a built-in firing pin.

Later on, we'll talk about what actually happens *inside* the ammunition cartridge once that primer has been struck.

As I mentioned earlier, the thing you wrap your hand around while shooting is the gun's grip (some folks call it a handle—which isn't necessarily wrong, but I like my students to know the proper names before going down their own path). The front of the grip (located right under the trigger guard) is called the front strap, and the back of the grip, the part that rests against your palm, is called the back strap. Follow the back strap up the back of the gun and you'll eventually reach the hammer—maybe.

In the old days, all revolvers had hammers because the hammers had firing pins attached.

So far in this chapter, I have mentioned single-action and double-action revolvers, but the advent of concealed carry revolvers gave birth to yet another category—double-action only.

Take a gander at the variety of revolvers in your local gun shop. Chances are, many of them will have no visible hammer whatsoever. Why? Because someone figured out that when you have a gun tucked into your pants, belt, pocket, or holster, you don't want it snagging on your clothing as you are retrieving it in haste. Hammer claws snag.

Many concealed carry revolvers have no visible hammer, which makes it easier to draw them from beneath clothing.

And so you have a generation of revolvers with no visible hammer or a "bobbed" hammer (with little or no spur—the part that you actually set your thumb on to cock it).

The revolvers with no hammer at all are "double-action only" (DAO)—which means you can't manually cock the hammer in order to lighten the trigger pull. Every pull is long and heavy

Guns with visible hammers aren't bad for carry purposes, but their hammer claws can snag on clothing at a most inconvenient time.

because the trigger is always doing twice the work—cocking *and* releasing the internal hammer.

In the next chapter, we'll talk about the pros and cons of DAO—and other—revolvers.

So, we've covered all the visible parts of your revolver, except for those blades, knobs, or grooves that sit atop the barrel. Those are your sights. They are essential on the range and in practice sessions—but you will probably not use them in a self-defense situation. But, learning to use them properly now will enhance your skill level and confidence down the road.

On most DAO revolvers, the sights are nothing more than nubbins—small bumps or ridges at the top back of the frame (near the hammer)—and a slim, metal blade atop the muzzle of the gun. Some models, such as the Ruger SP101, have variations with more defined notch sights at the back and a very visible fiber-optic sight in front. This type of sight configuration is much easier to see—but also creates more potential for snagging.

You can usually identify a carry gun, whether a revolver or semi-auto, by its pathetically tiny sights. These types of firearms are sometimes called "gut guns" because they simply aren't designed for target shooting. They are designed to have the smoothest possible

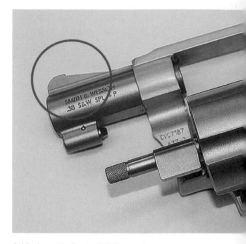

A blade-style front sight is most common on revolvers.

Other types of front sights can be more useful than the standard blade, such as glow-in-the-dark night sights or fiber-optic sights, like those shown here.

profile to allow for ease of concealment. When my buddy Mike bought a Ruger LCP, he told everyone, "I hate shooting this gun on the range, but that's not what it's designed for. It's here for me to yank out of my pocket, pull the trigger a couple times, and hand over to the police as evidence."

That pretty much summarizes the purpose of "gut guns," "poodle shooters," "mini me's," or whatever you want to call the smaller, concealable firearms with rounded edges and little-to-no sights.

SEMI-AUTOMATICS

So, if you have been holding your revolver and following along as we played "name those parts," you can set it down now and pick up your semi-automatic. It's going to look somewhat similar but there are some differences.

The parts they have in common include the barrel (and bore), muzzle, frame, trigger, trigger guard, front strap, back strap, grip, sometimes a hammer, and of course, the sights. But the way your semi-auto functions is vastly different from your revolver, even though the end result is the same.

The two types of guns obviously look rather different. The semi-auto is typically flatter and more squared off. Its barrel is sheathed beneath a slide that travels forward and back each time you fire the gun. That slide also comes in handy for minimizing recoil, so let's start there.

I tell my students that the slide of your semi-auto acts kind of like a shock absorber, taking some of the intensity of the recoil on itself as it moves rapidly forward and back. On a revolver, however, the only thing absorbing recoil is you!

When the slide slaps back, as it is doing in the photo, it absorbs a certain amount of the recoil. If you look carefully, you will see the ejected spent cartridge in the air above the gun.

Gun Girl Tip #14

While those spent casings aren't dangerous, they do fly out of the ejection port with a fair amount of speed, and, by the way, they are hot! I was shooting at the nearby Vandalia Range one afternoon, wearing one of my characteristic V-neck shirts. In the next shooting lane, a friend of mine was blasting away with his .45 ACP 1911. Now Fred stood about six feet eight inches in his bare feet, and, despite the presence of a high dividing wall, his shell casings kept sailing over the wall and pinging against the ground near my feet. I didn't think much about it until one of them sailed right down my shirt and nestled itself into my cleavage! I quickly set the safety on my gun and laid it down before doing a frantic dance (and exposing more than a little skin) as I tried to shake the casing out of my shirt. Needless to say, the hot metal left a nice little welt on my décolletage. So, ladies, when your instructor tells you to wear a crew neck shirt (or at least something that can be zipped up), it's a safety tip, not a fashion critique.

But the real purpose of the slide is to reload the gun after each shot. If you look at the slide on your semi-auto, you will notice it has an opening across the top and down the top right side. When the slide is closed, the opening is also closed off by the top of the chamber, but when you pull back the slide, that hole opens as it lines up with the chamber of the gun. If there is a round in the chamber when you pull the slide back, an internal extractor will yank the round out of the chamber as the ejector tosses it out of the gun through that hole, appropriately named the ejection port. Typically, all handguns eject to the right, so if you are standing to the right of someone who is shooting, be prepared to brush spent shell casings out of your hair—or wear a brimmed hat to help deflect the casings.

Inside the slide of your pistol, you may have a fixed barrel or a floating one. Most of them "float," which means they wiggle around a bit. That is not indicative of a problem. I can't count the number of times a customer has racked the slide back and jiggled the barrel indignantly—"Can you show me one that isn't broken?" I then gently explain that the barrel jiggles for a reason. As ammunition is loaded into the chamber of the gun, it slides up a "feed ramp" located at the back of the barrel. To make it easier for the ammunition to slide into the chamber, the front of the barrel tilts up slightly as the slide slaps backward, thus allowing the ammunition to easily glide up into the chamber. With a fixed barrel, you don't get that extra bit of assistance.

As with a revolver, your semi-auto has a grip. Unlike your revolver, that grip has a greater purpose than just something to hang on to! If you look at your gun, near where the trigger guard meets the grip, you will probably see a small button (unless you are using a Walther or a few other European models). That button—usually on the left side of the gun, but sometimes on both left and right—is the magazine release. The magazine is a metal or, occasionally, plastic piece that fits up into the hollowed-out grip. The magazine holds your pistol's ammunition. How much ammo it holds depends on the size and purpose of the gun itself.

A full-sized, high-end piece, such as a Springfield XD(M), will hold nineteen rounds in the magazine. A small, concealed carry model, such as a Sig Sauer P238, will hold six rounds, seven if you have the extended magazine.

The magazine snaps up into the hollowed-out grip of the gun.

This lever is alternately referred to as the slide stop or the slide release, depending on whether you are holding the slide open or snapping it closed.

If you press that button while holding your gun upright, gravity will do its job and the magazine will fall free from the grip. When you load the magazine with ammunition, you simply slap it into the hollow grip opening, making sure that it latches in place (if not, the ammo won't feed properly). The bullet end of the ammo will be pointing slightly upward and toward the muzzle, making it easy for the round to slide up the feed ramp and into the open chamber.

The magazine, by the way, has a taut spring coiled up inside it. That spring pushes a flat metal or plastic piece called the follower toward the

Gun Girl Tip #15

My friend Mike likes to teach his students "how to shoot yourself with an unloaded gun." It is a compelling lesson. Picking up a gun from the table, Mike racks the slide open and peers into the chamber. "Nope, it's empty," he says, flashing the empty chamber around to the class. With that, he pushes down on the slide stop, thus releasing the slide forward. Then, he carefully presses the magazine release, thus dropping the loaded mag safely onto the table. For extra effect—because this is serious stuff—he points the now magazine-free gun downrange and says, "There you have it—you have cleared the gun!" Then he presses the trigger. The resulting explosion from the muzzle scares the crap out of everyone (and momentarily deafens them, he discovered when he tried this exercise prior to donning ear protection). But it *does* get their attention. So, how did he fire the gun after carefully checking everything? Easy! He did things in the wrong order. You *always* drop the magazine first. If you rack the slide first and check the chamber (and you have a full magazine), the minute you release that slide back into a closed position, you will load a round from the magazine into the chamber. So, even if you drop the magazine, you have already done the damage.

top of the mag. You press down on the follower to load in the ammo (always remembering that the bullet end of the ammo points up slightly).

Just above where you typically find the magazine release, you'll see a square of metal resting on the frame and against the slide. This is your slide release—or slide stop, depending on what you are trying to do!

Most guns, though not all, have this nifty little piece. When you pull back on the slide (assuming an empty magazine is resting in the grip), the slide stop will hold the slide open so that you can inspect the interior of the firearm. However, if you have no magazine in your gun or if you have a *loaded* magazine in the gun, the slide stop will not engage. Thus, it is helpful to remove the magazine when you want to practice racking the slide repeatedly. If you have a loaded magazine in the gun, the slide stop will not only *not* catch the slide, but the forward motion of the slide will load a round into the chamber. So you *never* want to rack that slide with a loaded mag in place unless you intend to chamber a round.

Now, in recent years, many gun companies have introduced a magazine safety—which means that certain models will not fire if the magazine is not in place, even if there is a round in the chamber. This helps to prevent the incidence of people shooting themselves (or others) with "empty" guns. But this problem has by no means been eliminated, because many new models do not have that particular safety feature. Older guns, too, won't have it. So the best practice is to simply clear your gun (that is, rack open the slide and check the chamber for ammo) in the proper order, dropping the magazine *first*, then opening the chamber and peering in. Remember—if you have already dropped the magazine you will have to manually push up on the slide stop in order to lock back the slide. If you have arthritic thumbs like I do, that can be a challenge. But is it worth your life? Yeah. Of course it is!

In the case of my Springfield XD, the takedown lever flips up and the gun comes apart easily. Not every gun is so simple to take down.

Bear in mind that some guns, the Beretta Nano springs to mind, do not have external slide stops. Everything happens inside the gun, so you have to have an empty magazine shoved into the grip in order to hold open the slide. If you rack the slide on your Nano (or similar models) and it does not lock back, you either have no magazine in the grip or you have a loaded one!

Frequently, you will notice another button, lever, or bar located in front of the slide stop, resting in the gap between the frame and the slide. This is the takedown lever, which is flipped up (or down), depressed, or removed in order to take apart your gun for cleaning and maintenance. Since every gun is a little different, you will

The external, manual safety. Not every gun has (or needs) one, but for single-action semi-autos like the P238, they are a must if you plan to carry with a round in the chamber.

have a different takedown process for every firearm you own. But you can minimize your headaches three ways: (a) when purchasing the gun, ask your salesperson to walk you through the takedown process; (b) read the manual that accompanies your new firearm; and (c) get on YouTube and search for your gun and terms such as "cleaning" or "fieldstripping." If you do each of these things, you will quickly master the art of disassembling and assembling your gun. Be aware: The polymer-framed, striker-fired guns such as Glocks, Springfield XDs, and Smith & Wesson M&Ps (among others) are very easy to take apart. The classic 1911 models are a little more complex—easily mastered, but it will take a little more effort and a few additional salty words.

Lined up with the takedown lever and the slide stop, you may (or may not) see yet another lever or tab toward the back of the gun, along the top of the frame next to the slide. This is your external manual safety. The placement of a manual safety makes it easy for you to knock it off (that is, make the gun ready to fire) with a swipe of your dominant thumb, just as your index finger is beginning to depress the trigger.

There are a lot of misconceptions about manual safeties—the primary one being that they are a magical barrier between you and any kind of accidental discharge. As you will learn if you take the NRA's basic pistol course, "a safety is a mechanical device that can fail." You should never trust your safety to prevent an accident. Accidents are prevented by following the rules of safe gun handling, *not* by counting on a lever or button to remain in position. Revolvers, by the way, almost never have safeties—the only exception I can think of is the Heritage Rough Rider series of .22 plinking pistols.

There is also a tendency among beginners to shy away from guns such as Glocks, which have no external manual safety. Just last week, I waited on a gentleman who was looking for his first gun. Based on his specifications, I lined up a Glock, a Springfield, and a Smith & Wesson M&P on the counter in front of him, explaining how each gun functioned and how each might meet his needs. When I pointed out that the M&P had a manual safety, while the other two models did not, his eyes widened and he sniffed disdainfully. "Well then, of course, I don't want either of those. Who would buy a gun with no safety?"

Hmmmm—every police department in the country?

I explained that the absence of an external manual safety did *not* mean the absence of a safe firearm. "The striker-fired guns are inherently safe," I explained, "because the internal striker is held away from the ammunition cartridge until and unless you pull the trigger. Additionally,

Wrapping your hands around a Desert Eagle (the large gun) can be more challenging than doing so with an LC9.

there is a firing pin block that prevents any discharge in the event the gun is dropped."

I went on to point out the safety triggers on both the Glock and the Springfield, which are designed so you cannot inadvertently pull the trigger without proper finger placement. I also pointed to the grip safety on the Springfield and explained how a shooter must hold the gun properly or it will not discharge, no matter how many times you pull the trigger.

My customer glared at me like I was trying to sell him ten acres of swampland in Florida. "But there's no safety to turn on or off," he said, turning the Glock over in his hand. "That seems dangerous to me, and I don't intend to buy a dangerous gun."

He went on to purchase a more traditional model, one that is far more likely to discharge accidentally—but it had a manual safety and he felt good about that. Sometimes you just have to know when you've said all you can say. I did advise him to practice switching off the safety each and every time he shoots, so that, in a personal-defense situation, the necessary thumb movement will be instinctive.

You have to decide for yourself what you are comfortable with, but be assured that roughly three-quarters of our nation's policemen carry Glocks because they are safe firearms; they—and other similar striker-fired models—offer the most dependable design currently available. If law enforcement trust their lives to a particular model, then I am content that I can too.

Although we have already talked about the grip in various sections of this book, we have not addressed the fact that various grips have different

From left are two single-stack magazines. The farthest right is a double stack.

When you see screws in the grip panels, you know that the panels can be removed and replaced, as shown on my 1911.

textures and thicknesses. I picked up a .50 AE Desert Eagle made by Magnum Research the other day. Although I had fired one a few years ago (and kind of liked it), the gun is not one I would ever add to my wish list because I simply can't wrap my hands around it.

A customer was watching me and shook his head in confusion. "Why would anyone want a gun like that?" he asked.

I shrugged. "Intimidation? Bragging rights? Bear hunting?" I suggested.

He nodded thoughtfully and moved on down the counter. I was pleased that his question was about *want* and not *need*. Questioning why someone "needs" a particular gun usually precedes a unilateral decision that *no one* "needs" that particular model. I may not want or need a Desert Eagle, because it simply does not fit my lifestyle or physical ability to shoot the darned thing effectively. But I sure as heck don't intend to tell some six-foot-three guy who weighs three hundred pounds and lives in the wilds of Alaska that he doesn't *need* that gun.

I don't own a tactical rifle (erroneously referred to as an "assault rifle" by members of the media—and sometimes even by uninformed gun owners), but the day I determine that someone else doesn't "need" to own one is the same day that someone, somewhere decides that I don't *need* to own a Springfield XD or a Sig Sauer 1911. A tattered strip of paper hung on my desktop computer for many years that declared, "Liberty is the one thing you cannot have without first giving it to others." Guns are a case in point. I talk to too many gun owners who are willing to concede gun control measures against any model that they don't own. It doesn't work that way. You're either free or you're not. Period.

But I digress. My point about the Desert Eagle is that I can't flipping hold the darned thing! The grip is too thick because the ammo inside it is just too big! But not all grips with powerful ammo are impossible for small hands.

The Smith & Wesson MP comes with interchangeable backstraps for a variety of hand sizes.

The Ruger SR22 features two different grip sleeves that can accommodate different hand sizes.

The magazine, which locks up into the grip, typically comes in either single-stack (where the ammo is piled one on top of the other) or double-stack (where rounds are zigzagged inside the magazine, allowing for more rounds).

When you are talking *big* rounds, such as the .50 AE or the .45 ACP, they are usually found in a single-stack configuration, because double-stack would make for a *very* beefy grip. But smaller rounds, such as the .40 S&W and the 9mm, are frequently found in both single- and double-stack. If your hand won't fit around a thick grip, take a look at the ammo configuration in the magazine. If it is double-stack, then look around for a similar model but in a single-stack version (for example, Smith & Wesson offers its M&P models in a small, medium, and large double-stack version but also in the thinner M&P Shield single-stack). You will

A Hogue grip can replace the factory grip and make the gun easier to grasp.

find that the grip is much slimmer when the rounds are stacked on top of each other. The downside is that single-stack models hold fewer rounds.

But it isn't always the size of the ammo or its configuration inside the magazine that makes a grip hard to handle. Sometimes it's the panels on either side of the grip that are too big. When I was shooting my 1911 competitively, I had a lot of trouble getting my thumb to reach the magazine release in order to reload quickly. I simply couldn't do it without moving my whole hand and wasting plenty of precious seconds. My husband pointed out that I needed to try thinner panels. With the help of our shop's 1911 guru, Bob, I was able to find the perfect set, and suddenly, my beloved 1911 became much easier to manage.

Always check out the grip panels to see if they are removable before you decide a gun won't work for you—you'll know if you see screws in the panels that they can be removed.

But even with the poly-framed (a.k.a. plastic) models, such as Glock, Springfield, or Smith & Wesson's M&P, there are often ways to modify the size of the grip. Many models today come with interchangeable back straps (that snap into or out of the back of the grip and make it larger or smaller in the hand), and some even come with a couple different grip "sleeves" that can be slid over the structural foundation of the grip in order to create a larger or smaller hand piece, as with the Ruger SR22.

The bottom line is that just because you pick up the gun and it doesn't fit your hand, it doesn't mean it *can't* fit your hand! And even if it cannot be adjusted through a new back strap or side panels, if the grip is too small, you can always turn to the variety of Hogue brand grips (and many others) on the market.

Something else to note when it comes to grips: there are different textures or checkering available, and they all serve a purpose beyond simple decoration. But they are not all created equal.

My hands don't perspire much when I shoot, but I have had students who left salt stains on my gun because they sweated so much! If you are a

I favor the smooth grip on the Glock Gen3 models.

My husband likes the sandpaper-like stippled grip on the Gen4s.

sweaty shooter, you will likely prefer a gun that sticks in your hand by virtue of a textured grip. My Springfield XD has some texturing but is relatively smooth, especially when contrasted with my Gen4 Glock, which feels like industrial-grade sandpaper in my hand. Still, the Glock is great for outdoor range shooting on a hot day. No matter how damp you are, it stays put. My Springfield is a little slipperier; in a case like this, you can buy a rubber "glove" that slides over the grip and gives you more sticking power.

If you are a white-knuckle shooter (and many people are in the beginning), the etching and stippling that keeps the gun in place when you start to sweat can have an unpleasant side effect. Before buying a gun with a lot of checkering or texture, make sure you hold it for a few minutes and try squeezing your hands tightly around the grip. Now how does it feel? When you pull your hands away, do they look like you just pressed them into a waffle iron? Imagine how they will look and feel after an hour on the range. Take that into account as you select your gun.

Whether you are choosing a concealed carry gun or a home defense gun, pick something that is comfortable in your hand. If you don't like holding the gun, then you probably won't shoot it regularly. And if you don't shoot it regularly, you won't be prepared to use it instinctively when all your senses are going crazy and your motor skills are history.

One additional caution on the Gen4 Glocks: the stippled grip has a tendency to snag nylon. If you wear it tucked into your belt and with a T-shirt or light polo shirt over it, prepare for snags. That doesn't mean the gun is hard to retrieve, it just means that the material on your shirt could be full of dimples and runs when you undress. Not something guys worry much about, but ladies tend to be a bit more finicky (and our clothes tend to cost more too!).

When you are trying out a handgun, be sure to ask questions about the grip: Are there interchangeable back straps? Is there a smaller model (like the M&P Shield)? Does this particular model come with a different texture? Most Glocks come in a Gen3 and a Gen4. I like the smoother grip of the Gen3. My husband prefers the stippled Gen4.

Gun parts are not always as they appear or, at least, may have additional components that will make a specific model more user-friendly for you. You just need to ask!

So that completes our detailed tour of your firearms, both revolver and semi-automatic. There are plenty of internal parts we could discuss, but, if you're like me, you want some time to soak in the basics. That's the purpose of this book: familiarizing you with the basics.

CHAPTER SUMMARY

- On double-action revolvers, the cylinder swings out on a crane, allowing you to load it and then lock it back into the frame.

- Single-action revolvers typically load through a loading gate, one round at a time. Or, you can remove the entire cylinder from the frame, load it, and then reconnect it to the frame.

- Rifling in the bore of the gun causes a bullet to spin so that it is aerodynamically stable in flight.

- The frame of the gun is the torso, off of which everything else hangs.

- In a modern double-action revolver, the act of pulling the trigger both cocks and releases the hammer.

- Most concealed carry revolvers do not have a visible hammer spur, in order to prevent snagging on clothing.

- A semi-automatic firearm features a slide that moves rapidly backward and forward, stripping a round of ammo out of the magazine and reloading the chamber after each shot.

- The spent casing from the fired round is pulled from the chamber by an extractor and ejected out of the ejection port.

- The slide release, or slide stop, locks the slide open so you can inspect the chamber of the gun (or releases the slide so that it slaps shut).

- A safety is a mechanical device that can fail—and a gun that does not have an external manual safety is not necessarily unsafe. Make sure you understand what the internal safety systems are before you jump to conclusions.

- The magazine locks into place inside the grip of the gun.

- Magazines may be double-stack or single-stack, with double-stack creating a larger grip and single-stack being narrower.

- The checkering or etching on the grip of a gun can help it stick in your hand better, but it can also be uncomfortable, especially when combined with the force of recoil.

CHAPTER 6

CHOOSE THE MODEL, STYLE, AND DESIGN FOR *YOU*

So now you know a little something about how guns work, and what all those parts and pieces do. Now you have to decide what style and model will work best for you. Or, perhaps you are still debating whether a gun is truly the right choice for you.

No one can make that decision for you. If you have a significant other or family member who is hell-bent on putting a gun in your hands, that's okay—as long as *you* have the final say. If you aren't quite ready to decide—and especially if you are *certain* you don't want a gun—then stand up and say no.

As a gun advocate, the last thing I want is for people who are uneasy, or downright scared, around firearms to be buying and using them. Hesitation and awkwardness with a gun are natural emotions in a beginning shooter, but if they are the result of a deep-seated anti-gun conviction, then you have no business using one, and, in fact, you'll likely do more harm than good.

I tell my students that almost every hesitation or fear can be overcome—except a fundamental refusal to use the gun for its intended purpose. Again, before you buy a gun for personal defense, ask yourself one serious question: Can I point this gun at another human being and pull the trigger?

If your answer is no—or even "I don't know"—then you probably aren't ready for your first gun. In fact, you may never be. Buy a big dog or a can of mace.

If you decide to own a gun and you don't believe, in your heart of hearts, that you can shoot another human being, then there's a good chance that your gun will be taken away from you and used against you. That's something no one wants, especially this lady who is telling you that guns are a great personal investment!

And yes, I truly believe in the value of firearms. I love owning them, shooting them, and teaching their safe use, but not everyone is prepared for gun ownership. When my friend Mike started taking me to the range, I was content to rent guns and shoot his. As time passed and I grew more confident in my own skill and knowledge, I knew that I could competently and safely own a firearm. I also gained the confidence that I could aim and fire it at anyone who was threatening me or my son.

If you are at that point as well, then it is time to talk about what gun is the best one to start with. My goal here is not to steer you to a particular model, though I certainly have my favorites, but, rather, to give you an idea of what works for your needs, size, lifestyle, and pocketbook!

REVOLVER VERSUS SEMI-AUTOMATIC

First of all, have you answered that very first "which style" question yet: revolver or semi-automatic? There are arguments on both sides, and, although I am a devoted semi-auto gal, I try to present both sides fairly. Why do I prefer semi-autos over revolvers? Absolutely *no* good reason—other than I just like them and I like the challenge of using them, cleaning them, and understanding how all the parts work together.

I also contend that certain semi-auto models offer much lighter recoil than a revolver that is similar in size and caliber. But not everyone agrees. I recently had a student who was undecided on her gun of choice. I ran her through about fifteen different models and she kept coming back to revolvers.

"I don't understand why you don't like them," she said, confused. "I don't notice any difference in the recoil between these revolvers and all those semi-autos."

I had taken her through all my go-to semi-autos that leave most students gasping in awe and appreciation. Not this lady. She held tight to her concealable revolver saying, "If I can't tell a difference, then I probably ought to go with the one that is easiest to use."

I couldn't argue with that logic. And I didn't even try.

And the truth is that a revolver *is* easier to load and use—with nowhere near as many external working parts. And, if there happens to be an ammunition malfunction (very rare), all you do is pull the trigger

The Ruger LCR is a moderately priced and reasonably concealable revolver.

again and allow the cylinder to cycle to the next chamber and the next round of ammo.

On the other hand, revolvers hold fewer rounds on average and can (no matter what my student thought) have more significant recoil when compared to a similar size and caliber semi-automatic.

Still, if you are looking for simplicity, you'll find it with a revolver. If you also want concealability, you will find it in such smaller, lighter models as the Smith & Wesson Airweight or the Ruger LCR. In fact, those who are torn between the price and convenience of the 9mm cartridge (usually reserved for semi-autos) and the simplicity of a revolver, can now experience the best of both worlds with Ruger's 9mm LCR. The disadvantage is the need for moon clips, which prevent the rimless 9mm cartridge from slipping through the cylinder chamber and falling out the front end.

I have a tendency to misplace moon clips because, well, they are small and flat, which means they easily slip into the nooks of my gun case or range bag. But it is a great addition to the LCR line, which now comes in .22 LR, .22 WMR, .38 Special, .357 Magnum, and 9mm.

If you are a die-hard revolver fan but simply cannot stomach the recoil of .38s and the like, I would also suggest a second look at the .22 WMR (also known as the .22 Magnum) caliber revolvers. While I don't advocate the .22 as a defensive round, I'd rather see you carry a revolver chambered in .22 Magnum versus .22 LR—and I'd rather see you carry a .22 of *any* type versus no gun at all.

I owned and used the Ruger LCR .38 Special for a while, mainly because I felt it was important to have experience with a variety of models. I liked the rubber grip on the LCR (with comfortable finger cuts) and the fact that Ruger built a gel pack into the back strap, which helps to reduce the felt recoil. It was, admittedly, a simple gun to carry and use. But, in the end, I traded it in on a semi-automatic.

SEMI-AUTOMATICS

If you share my appreciation for autoloaders (a.k.a. semi-automatics) and want to push yourself a little outside your comfort zone, then I would recommend getting comfortable with one of the many truly awesome magazine-fed handguns currently on the market.

Which one you choose is truly a matter of personal choice. As you become more familiar with firearms, you'll have your favorites.

I still own my Springfield XD 9mm that I bought right after qualifying for my concealed carry permit. But I have added new guns to the mix along the way, sold some, and kept others.

I like a gun that has a lighter (but not unsafe) trigger pull. But if it's going to be in my purse or on my belt, I don't want the trigger to be too easy to pull. I like a gun with a slide that is pretty easy to rack. For carry purposes, I like a gun that is lightweight but not so lightweight that it kicks the heck out of my hands!

So, what are my favorite carry guns? Well, I love the Glock 42 and 43—light to carry, crisp trigger pull, and manageable slide. Like the original Glocks, they have a polymer frame—the ol' "Tupperware gun" that many mocked when Glock introduced its "plastic" guns in the 1980s. Like all the past and current Glock models, they shoot like a dream. I would trust my life to it, as so many law enforcement officials have done in the past and continue to do. Pricewise, this slender .380 (Glock 42) and 9mm (Glock 43) runs in the middle. Not cheap but also not pricey by most firearms standards. My husband carries both, and I am always borrowing them for a little range time.

Gun Girl Tip #16

Gun names and calibers can get pretty confusing. My students routinely confuse caliber with model number. Most guns will have a manufacturer name (Ruger), a model name or number (LCR), and a caliber (.38 Special, 9mm, .22 LR, etc.). So you might reference this gun in conversation as "a Ruger LCR .38." Some guns are numbered instead of named, such as the Glock 17, 19, 22, 27, etc. Those numbers have nothing to do with the caliber. A Glock 22 is a .40-caliber weapon and a Glock 17 is a 9mm, whereas a Ruger SR22 really is a .22 LR. You'll eventually get more comfortable with all the names and numbers, but it is a little confusing in the beginning. In chapter 7, I talk about the names and numerical designations for ammunition— and why they are every bit as confusing as they seem!

My full-sized Springfield XD is a perfect home defense gun with a manageable recoil. It's also a moderately priced gun.

The Glock 42 is a lightweight .380 that offers the solid construction and dependability that Glock is known for. The newer Glock 43 accomplishes the same thing as a 9mm.

My current carry gun, the Sig P238, is not lightweight compared to a polymer-framed model, but it's got a light trigger pull, an easy slide to rack, and a very manageable recoil.

I carry a Sig Sauer P238, also a .380, designed by Sig to look pretty much like John Browning's famed 1911. The slide is a breeze to rack, even for arthritic fingers. The trigger offers a gentle single-action pull, and the recoil is minimal for a gun that size. The gun comes in a vast array of styles (everything from my basic stainless steel model to rainbow or fuchsia). The only thing this fun little pistol lacks is a gentle price tag. I paid $649 for mine and that was a couple years ago. One downside: it is, like its big brother the 1911, a single-action firearm, which means you must have the external manual safety on at all times if you plan to carry with a round in the chamber. If a round is chambered but the safety is *not* activated, you have a live round just waiting for the cocked hammer to fall, something easily achieved if the gun is bouncing around in your purse or pocket. If you can't remember to set the safety each and every time you chamber a round to carry, don't buy this gun or don't carry with a round chambered (which means you will have to remember to rack the slide and chamber a round before firing the gun).

At the lower end of the price spectrum, I am fond of

Kel-Tec's P-11. It's a 9mm that is larger (and more powerful) than either the Glock 42 or the Sig. It's got a polymer frame that makes it carryable but, with a double-stack magazine, it is a bit bulkier than the single-stack Glock 43 or the Sig P938 (the 9mm brother of the P238). It also has a more powerful recoil, but it's not really too bad for a small 9mm. There's nothing sleek or sexy about the P-11—it is a utility gun, plain and simple—but what the Kel-Tec lacks in dazzle it makes up for in price. It's about half the cost of the Glock and almost a third of the cost of the Sig.

A Kel-Tec P11 is a low-cost carry firearm with a manageable recoil.

I am also a fan of the Smith & Wesson M&P Shield 9mm for carry purposes. And the new Ruger LC9 striker-fired version has a lot to offer, as well. Heck, if you pinned me down, there are very few handguns I don't like. But there are plenty that don't work for me personally.

I wasn't crazy about the Ruger LC9 until they came out with a striker-fired model. The trigger pull is much more comfortable, and the gun is very concealable.

That's the secret to selecting the right gun for you. I can tell you what I like and what is well made—and you may agree with me—but the gun has to work for you.

When you are gazing at potential firearms in your local gun shop, make sure you take them out of the case and hold them. See how your hand fits the grip. Both hands, in proper

This gun is clearly too big for those hands— the backs of the hands should be touching. The grip should not be visible in between.

shooting position, should cover the grip and not leave much showing through your thumbs. If there is a substantial amount of visible grip, then the gun doesn't really fit your hand. If the opposite is true and your hands seem to be flopping over each other, then the gun is likely too small.

In the case of a revolver, make sure your hands don't stick out in front of the cylinder. Otherwise you could end up with a nasty burn from the hot gasses that escape the cylinder upon firing!

It's pretty easy to tell if a firearm is too small for your hand. Especially with a revolver, you want to make sure your fingers aren't near the front of the cylinder, where they could be burned by hot gasses.

As you hold a semi-automatic, try using the thumb on your dominant hand to drop the magazine by depressing the button at the point where the trigger guard meets the grip. If you can do so easily, without having to twist your hand position, that's a good thing. If you are in a personal defense situation and you have to reload quickly, the last thing you want is to have to contort your hands into new (nonfiring) positions while you drop and reload your mags.

FIT AND TRIGGER PULL

Next, lay your index finger along the frame and see where it falls in relation to the trigger. Do you have to bend your finger substantially in order to set the pad of your index finger on the trigger? Then your fingers may be too long for the gun. Conversely, if the pad of your finger barely reaches the trigger, you may have trouble summoning the strength to pull it. Bear in mind that most concealed carry guns have a long,

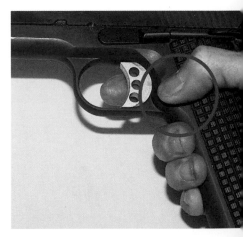

Try using your thumb to make sure you can drop the magazine without contorting your hand. This is essential if you must reload quickly.

heavy trigger pull. It's one of the safety measures that prevent you from accidentally depressing the trigger while it's bouncing around in your purse, pocket, holster, etc. If you plan to carry, don't expect a feather-light trigger pull (especially from a gun with no external manual safety).

So, your desired firearm fits your hand well? Great! Now try pulling the trigger a few times—slowly. Don't yank it; just give it a gentle backward press toward you. If you have to struggle to pull it, hand the gun back to the nice salesman and keep on looking.

Gun Girl Tip #17

While a semi-automatic has a slide that covers the actual barrel, the barrel of a revolver is more exposed. Because a barrel heats up as you fire the gun, you have to be especially careful with a revolver not to grab the barrel after you've put a couple dozen rounds through it.

And please don't feel guilty about handling a bunch of guns. Any gun shop worth its salt is going to want to help you make the best possible choice. As a gun salesperson, I must admit that it's kind of nice when someone comes up to the counter, points to a particular model, and says, "Hand me the paperwork—that's what I want!" No muss, no fuss. But, from a satisfaction standpoint, nothing beats working with someone step by step and helping them find something that really meets their needs! If you are shopping in a gun store that dissuades browsing or makes you feel uneasy when you ask to see more than a couple guns, turn around and march back out again. Don't waste your money on them. Buying a gun is serious business, and anyone who doesn't treat it that way shouldn't be rewarded with your hard-earned cash.

Once you have determined whether the trigger pull is manageable, take a minute and try racking the slide several times (see chapter 4 for a description of how to do it properly). Before you assume that the slide is too stiff for you to manage, make sure you are racking it properly. I'd be the first to tell you that there are slides that my arthritic hands just can't rack easily, but I refuse to let the gun get the better of me. I'll get that slide racked no matter how much my thumbs hurt in the process—but any gun that puts me through that much pain will never come to live at my house!

Some of the slides I am partial to include those on most Glocks, the Sig P238 and P938, the Walther PK380, and .22s such as the Ruger SR22 and the Walther P22. If you are an older shooter or just have weak hands, you may want to try these models to see if one of them works for you. But remember, if you are buying a concealed carry gun, it will be smaller—and more difficult to get a good grip on the short, narrow slide.

And speaking of small guns, pretty much every day someone comes into the shop seeking a concealed carry gun. And, invariably, some of them complain about the fact that their pinky fingers don't quite fit on the grip of the gun. The bottom line is that these pieces are designed to be concealable—they will naturally be smaller in your hand than the "tweener" (in-between sized) and larger models. Yes, they are a bit harder to hold onto, but when you start adding extended magazines, Hogue grips, etc., you also detract from the concealability aspect, which is why you are buying that particular model to begin with!

Yes, you have to find the gun that feels right for you, but you also have to be sure it will serve its intended purpose. A concealed carry gun that has been tricked out with extenders and expanders is just a Franken-gun that may give you what you want but won't necessarily give you what you need.

Now, before you plop down a handful of cash on your dream gun, you may still be pondering a few things—such as its color, perhaps. Both revolvers and semi-autos these days come in a variety of shades, ranging from rainbow to "Pepto pink" to camo and more. Me—I am a "basic black" girl. I'd rather be known for my accuracy than my color coordination. But I have sold guns to a number of ladies who favor making a bold statement—and there's nothing wrong with that.

My only caution would be with regard to concealability. I find that a matte black finish stays concealed more effectively, even when your sweatshirt rides up a bit or your pocket sags open for a moment. Nobody seems to notice the thin chunk of black metal and plastic hiding in the shadows. Not so for polished stainless steel, iridescent rainbow, or blinding fuchsia.

Now the truth is that most people who don't carry don't notice the telltale bulges on those who do. But a wrong twist or turn can reveal a purple pistol or a red revolver a bit more readily than a basic black one. And, yes, there are people—more than you may realize—who would gleefully call the cops to report someone nearby "who has a gun"!

By the way, in the event that ever happens, the appropriate response is to greet the police with a calm demeanor, hand them your concealed carry permit, and do whatever it is they ask of you. It is never smart to argue with people who (a) are aware you are carrying a weapon and (b) have the authority to shoot you if you appear to be a threat.

Now I am not saying that your periwinkle revolver will get you shot or arrested—only that it could be more visible. And, in the end, concealed means concealed: your gun should stay that way unless and until it is necessary to defend yourself.

So perhaps, by now, you have decided whether you want a revolver or a semi-automatic. And perhaps you have even decided which specific model. Hopefully, before you drain your bank account, you will find a way to try out your dream gun on the range. The proof is in the shooting, and only then will you know for certain if your "perfect gun" really is perfect for you.

But if you find yourself torn between a couple different models, you can always consider buying more than one gun. In fact, I can almost guarantee that, no matter what you say now, you will eventually own more than one gun. It just goes with the territory (remember my shoe analogy in chapter 1?). Indeed, you may even decide to *carry* more than one gun. Sound crazy? I know plenty of folks who have a standard mid-sized concealed carry gun on their hips and a convenient "poodle shooter" strapped to their ankles. Off-duty or retired cops, in particular, like to be well armed, but plenty of law-abiding citizens feel likewise.

My favorite "two-gun story" isn't entirely a concealed carry story, but it does underscore the effectiveness of a hidden firearm—and it also emphasizes that "peace through strength" is not a concept limited to world powers.

My late ex-father-in-law, a.k.a. Pop, was a retired army lieutenant colonel and a tough guy with a heart of gold. His hardscrabble upbringing in America's great Northwest had seen him leave a troubled home life at the tender age of twelve. He eventually joined the military in the final days of World War II, put himself through college at Ohio University in Athens, Ohio, and ultimately became a successful businessman in Dayton, Ohio, and the proud papa of six sons, with his wife Maggie. When the family moved from the city to a farm in rural Warren County during the late 1960s, they discovered that a few of their neighbors were less *Green Acres*-style oddballs and more hostile hill folk—along the lines of the disreputables that parade through FX's acclaimed Kentucky-based cop drama, *Justified*.

Down the road from the Engels' Telegraph Mills Farm lived a fellow named Jeb who was rumored to have been not simply a Klansman but the Grand Dragon of the local Klan chapter. Locals spoke in hushed tones about the many "accidental" fires that had consumed the homes of those who had incurred the wrath of Jeb.

Shortly after arriving in the rural community, Pop was out walking his eighty-three-acre farm one afternoon, toting a beautiful (and expensive) 1916 Parker V grade shotgun, just in case a rabbit crossed his path or he stumbled across wild dogs, coyotes, or some other menacing critter. And so he did—Jeb. Now Jeb was trespassing, of course, but that didn't matter to ol' Jeb. He struck up a conversation with Pop, who questioned him casually about what he was doing on the property.

"Oh I don't mean no harm, sir." Jeb grinned. "I was just passin' through. That's okay, isn't it?"

Pop made it clear that passing through was one thing, but hunting the property without permission was not. Jeb grinned and nodded amicably, before setting his gaze on the Parker.

"Well now, Mr. Engel, that's a mighty fine-looking shotgun you have there. Mind if I take a look at it?"

Pop handed Jeb the gun and slipped a hand into his jacket, smiling good-naturedly the whole time.

Jeb turned the gun over in his hands and made admiring sounds. Then his gaze narrowed and he looked at Pop. "Yessir, this is a mighty nice gun. What are you going to do if I just decide to keep it?"

Pop snorted a quick chuckle and stared straight back at him. "Well, Jeb, then I guess I'd just have to blow a giant hole in you with the .38 revolver I'm holding."

The reaction was swift and immediate.

"Oh now, no need for that. I was just kidding," he said, handing the Parker back to its owner. "Welcome to the neighborhood. I'm sure we're gonna get along fine."

Pop laughed about that encounter until the day he died. More important, it drove home a lesson about preparation and the value of a hidden gun.

Later in life, Jeb tried to rehabilitate himself several times by becoming a woodworker and later a horseman. He was still Jeb, however, and still raised the Confederate flag outside his house each morning—and still proudly referred to himself as "briarhopper Amish."

But what struck me was that any time I ran across him, he always nodded deferentially and asked about my father-in-law's well-being. Jeb would smile and cluck his teeth and say, "Yep, that John Engel is a standup guy and a true deeplomat"—thus underscoring another important lesson: no one ever won over a potential enemy with weakness. Jeb never pestered Pop or any other member of the family, nor did any of Jeb's many minions. They all understood that everyone on Telegraph Mills

Farm was armed—and fully prepared to defend themselves. Amazing how neighborly that made them!

So having more than one gun within reach isn't a bad idea. And, if you are undecided on whether you would prefer a revolver or a semi-automatic, there are plenty of good reasons to own both.

Don't hesitate to ask your friendly local gun salesperson about the advantages and disadvantages of each model from his perspective. He (or she) can also school you in the hidden cost of buying a gun—the cost of the ammunition. Not only do different calibers cost more to produce but, in this day and age, there are shortages, depending on what the public is hoarding at any given time and which calibers or models the government is threatening to ban.

ACTIONS

As you weave your way through the various types of handguns, you will encounter terms such as single-action, double-action, double-action only (or DAO), double/single-action, and safe-action, also known as striker-fired. All these terms relate directly to the work performed by the trigger. In the old days, pulling the trigger simply meant releasing the hammer forward so that its firing pin could strike the ammo's primer cup and discharge a bullet. But today, a trigger may perform a variety of duties, ranging from both cocking and releasing the hammer to deactivating internal safeties to compressing and releasing a spring that sends a firing pin forward into the primer.

As you shop, you will encounter the following designations. Understand what they are and how they impact the ease with which you use your handguns.

SINGLE-ACTION

A single-action (SA) trigger performs the *single action* of releasing the hammer forward to strike the primer cup and discharge the weapon. Early revolvers in the old West were single-action and required that cowboys and gunslingers recock the gun each time before firing (typically by yanking backwards on the hammer claw with a thumb). If you are looking for a gun that will serve you well in a personal defense situation, a single-action revolver isn't it. Most single-actions today are plinking guns, such as the Ruger Single-Six and the Heritage Rough Rider, both .22 LR and/or .22 Magnum. Other, higher-caliber revolvers, such as Ruger's Blackhawk, Uberti's Cattleman, or the Beretta Stampede, are typically intended to be modern replicas of revered firearms like the Colt Peacemaker, "the gun that won the West." These typically .44 Magnum,

.357 Magnum, and .45 Long Colt models are used for hunting, collecting, cowboy re-enacting, and other sporting activities. The advantage to a single-action gun is that the trigger pull is very crisp and comfortable because the trigger is only performing one job—releasing the manually cocked hammer. Single-action revolvers are rarely, however, used for personal defense, unless, of course, they are all you have available when someone attacks you. They are beautiful guns and certainly evoke memories of our nation's frontier beginnings, but they are not something you drop into your purse and carry around.

There are, however, single-action guns that you can carry; they just aren't revolvers. While a single-action revolver must be manually cocked by one's thumb against the hammer spur, a single-action semi-automatic reflects the brilliance of gun genius John Moses Browning, who arguably created the most famous firearm in history when he built the 1911. Guns made in the 1911 style *are* single-action, but you don't have to manually rack the slide or cock the hammer each time you want to fire. Why? Because Browning's design relies on the slide (which moves back and forth to eject and reload cartridges) to smack into the hammer, thereby recocking it to fire again. On a semi-automatic single-action, the slide does the work that your thumb is forced to do on a revolver. As a result, single-action semi-autos such as the Kimber Ultra Carry, Springfield EMP, or Sig P238 and P938 are very popular personal defense guns that are designed to be carried "cocked and locked" (that is, with a round chambered, the hammer cocked, and the safety on). As with all single-action firearms, the trigger pull on these guns is much lighter than double-action models, because the trigger only has one task: to release the hammer.

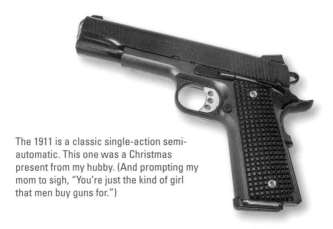

The 1911 is a classic single-action semi-automatic. This one was a Christmas present from my hubby. (And prompting my mom to sigh, "You're just the kind of girl that men buy guns for.")

DOUBLE-ACTION

A double-action handgun is sometimes called double-action only (DAO) to prevent confusion with double-action/single-action (DA/SA) designs, but only some double-action handguns are double-action only. Double-action refers to the work done by the trigger—that is, that it performs two tasks versus a single one.

In a double-action revolver with an exposed hammer, you no longer have to cock the hammer with your thumb, because the internal trigger mechanism both cocks and releases the hammer. Now, the nice thing about an exposed hammer double-action revolver is that you can simply pull the trigger until you have discharged all the rounds in the cylinder *or* you can enjoy a much lighter trigger pull by manually cocking the hammer as yesterday's cowboys would have done with their single-action only models. Are you with me? That's the advantage of having a traditional revolver with a double-action design. The disadvantage, of course, is that hammer spurs snag on loose clothing if your goal is to carry. Hence the introduction of hammerless revolvers, which are, in fact, genuine DAO handguns. They are DAO because there is no other option. Without an exposed hammer, there is nothing to cock. The disadvantage of these carryable pieces is that the trigger pull is longer and heavier and you have no means to lighten it. But double-action revolvers are very popular carry guns, both with and without hammers. Models such as the Ruger LCR, Smith & Wesson Airweight, and the Charter Arms Pink Lady are among the top sellers in our nation, especially among novice shooters.

There are also plenty of double-action/DAO semi-automatic pistols such as the Ruger LC9, the Smith & Wesson Bodyguard, and the Kel-Tec PF-9. The heavy trigger pull of the double-action design makes these guns a good choice for concealed carry purposes. Since it requires pressure to pull the trigger, these models lend themselves to bouncing around in pockets or purses and on ankles or waists. As always, try the trigger pull to make sure you can manage it. I've processed several trade-ins on Bodyguards, not because it's a bad gun but because someone bought it based on its size and how it felt in their hands—without ever pulling that trigger.

"It's such a cute little gun," one lady told me. "I guess I just assumed it would be easy to shoot."

DOUBLE-ACTION/SINGLE-ACTION

This type of gun is only found in the semi-auto design, and it combines the best of both worlds: the long, heavy (and thus safe) trigger pull of a double-action pistol on the first shot, followed by the lighter, easier

The Beretta M9, used by the military, is one of the best known DA/SA style guns.

single-action pull for all subsequent shots. The Sig P226 and SP2022 are popular examples of the DA/SA style. One of the best known of the DA/SA firearms is the Beretta M9, which has been the sidearm of choice for the United States military since they moved away from the 1911 style in 1986. While the M9 is not a concealed carry gun (unless you are very large and have similarly large pockets and baggy clothing), I would trust it to perform well in a home defense scenario. But before you run out and buy one (or the civilian version known as a 92FS), make sure you give it a live-fire test flight. That initial DA trigger pull is fairly stout, and if you can't successfully make that first pull, then the ease and comfort of subsequent single-action pulls is completely immaterial.

STRIKER-FIRED OR SAFE-ACTION

"Safe-action" is the term coined by Glock for its revolutionary striker system that mechanically blocks the firing pin from moving forward until and unless the trigger is completely depressed. Three separate internal safeties are released and reset by the trigger pull, giving the Glock and its many imitators "the hardest-working trigger in the gun business." Yet the resulting weight of the pull is amazingly crisp and comfortable. No, it is not as light as your typical single-action pull, but it's a darned sight better than most double-action designs.

Your best bet is to do your homework, try out a variety of guns—both pistols and revolvers: double-action, single-action, safe-action, and everything in between—talk to your fellow gun owners (but bear in mind that we all have our biases), and think seriously about what you want and need. Do this and—as with cars, mates, and houses—you may be lucky enough to find "the one" that suits you perfectly, lives up to all your expectations, and doesn't cost too much to maintain.

As I suggested earlier, modern technology can assist the process if you take advantage of the many instructional videos available on YouTube. But you should approach each one with the understanding that anyone can make and post a video. The best ones will come from credible resources such as the National Shooting Sports Foundation (NSSF), individual gun manufacturers, or the NRA.

I just finished watching one especially detestable amateur video where an Andrew Dice Clay wannabe attempted to guide people through their first visit to a gun shop, first by insulting all gun shop customers and then by explaining that most gun salespeople hate first-time buyers. What? Throughout this book I try to underscore the importance of finding a retailer who is willing to take the time necessary to educate you and give you a positive sales experience. Don't compromise there. They do exist, no matter what this video Neanderthal claims.

You will be well served by doing your gun shopping in a reputable retail establishment. I have a special preference for the "mom and pop" shops because they give directly back to the community, but even a well-established big-box store is a solid option. The rationale here is more pragmatic than civic. Guns do break; sometimes you break them, sometimes they roll off the assembly line with issues. More often, nothing major is wrong but you need guidance on the mechanics of your firearm. No matter the case, you have no handy resource when you purchase online, at a gun show, or from an individual. If there is a problem with your gun, you'll be stuck going straight through the manufacturer, which can be difficult and frustrating. A local retailer will normally run interference between you and the manufacturer in addition to offering advice, guidance, and minor repairs or upgrades, as needed. When you develop a relationship with a local gun shop, you will always have expert opinions and insight at your disposal. Chapter 10 will offer suggestions on how to go about finding such a place.

CHAPTER SUMMARY

- *You* should always make the final decision regarding the make, model, and caliber of firearm that best suit your needs. Welcome input from friends, family, and sales people, but decide for yourself what—and whether—you will shoot.

- Revolvers offer simplicity but don't always have manageable recoil.

- Semi-autos are more complex but typically carry many more rounds and have less recoil, greater concealability, and a broader selection of styles.

- Always make sure your gun of choice fits your hand properly—that your index finger can reach the trigger, that you can press the mag release without changing your hand position, and that you can effectively rack the slide.

- Trigger pull weight varies from gun to gun. Make sure the pull is comfortable and manageable for you.

- Colorful guns may make a statement, but they are not necessarily good carry guns because they are more easily detected.

- Single-action revolvers must be manually cocked (pressing thumb to hammer spur) before each shot, while a single-action semi-auto is recocked by the backward movement of the slide.

- Buying your gun from a brick-and-mortar retailer can be an advantage if it breaks or requires maintenance because you have somewhere local to take it, versus sending the gun back to the manufacturer.

CHAPTER 7

PRAISE THE LORD AND PASS THE AMMUNITION

It is rare that you will hear me say that Europeans do something better than Americans. I am pretty patriotic about this nation and all that we have achieved in a relatively short period of time—but when it comes to ammunition names and designations, I have to tip my hat to our brothers and sisters across the pond.

I spent my early days as a shooter thoroughly confused by ammunition—wondering about the differences between 9mm, 9mm Largo, 9mm Parabellum, 9mm NATO, 9x19, 9mm short, 9mm Luger, and 9mm Makarov; wondering if a .357 Magnum would fire in a gun chambered for .357 Sig; wondering why a .45 Colt and a .45 ACP round wouldn't fire from the same gun.

I puzzled over the function of ball-tip rounds, hollow-points, +P, +P+, wadcutters, semi-wadcutters, and the hundreds of other makes, models, and designations until my poor little head nearly exploded.

Then I learned that the first rule of American ammunition is "don't waste time trying to make sense of something that makes no sense!"

While the Europeans measure the dimensions of almost all of their ammunition in millimeters (diameter x length), we Americans seem to name ammo the same cavalier way we might name a pet—based on whatever tickles our fancy on that particular day.

First of all—remember all those 9mm variants I named in the first paragraph? Well, with the exception of 9mm Largo, 9mm short, and 9mm Makarov, they are all the same round! Yep, the box of ammo you buy for

A 9 is not a 9 is not a 9. Sometimes it's a Luger (bottom box and cartridge at right), and sometimes it's a Makarov or a Kurz or a Largo. Make sure you know what you are buying.

your standard American 9mm pistol may be labeled 9x19, 9mm, 9mm Parabellum, 9mm Luger, or 9mm NATO. Why? Well, because that's what the manufacturer decided to call it.

The Europeans do it a little more wisely—they use that pesky metric system on everything. In Europe, our .380 ACP round (also known as a 9mm short or a 9mm Kurz) is simply a 9x17, our typical 9mm round is a 9x19, and so on.

But here in America, we're an independent bunch and we do things however we want, mixing metrics with decimal inches, manufacturer names, and descriptors of all shapes and sizes. And thus, ammo becomes a confusing morass of names and numbers. For example, you have probably heard of the rifle round known as the .30-06? I always ask my students to tell me what caliber it is. A few cautiously venture that it is, perhaps, a .30-caliber. I praise them for their insight before asking what the aught six means. And suddenly the room falls silent. The aught six, I tell them, is simply the year that the round was first manufactured. In all of my classes, only one student has ever guessed correctly!

"Okay guys," I continue, "now that we know *that*, anyone care to guess what a .45-70 is?"

Once more, they venture a guess that it is a .45-caliber round. Right again! More confident now, they cautiously suggest that the 70 means the round was first manufactured in 1970.

"You'd think that wouldn't you," I say, "but, in fact, it refers to the grains of black powder that were once used in that round. We don't even use black powder anymore in manufacturing .45-70 ammo, but the name stuck."

Similarly, your revolver might use a .357 Magnum cartridge but if you try to put .357 Sig ammo into it, you won't have much success when you pull the trigger.

Of course when you go buy a cleaning kit for your .357 Magnum revolver, you will discover that your kit will clean not only the .357 but also the .38 Special, the .380 ACP, and the 9mm. Why? Because they are all the same diameter—different lengths and shapes and charges, mind you, but all the same bore size. Still, you *can't* use them interchangeably.

A .38 Special compared to the slightly larger (but same diameter) .357 Magnum.

Well, except in the case of .357 Magnums and .38 Specials. When I encounter someone who wants to buy a revolver for personal protection, I often encourage them to consider a .357 Magnum. The .357 Magnum round is frequently viewed as the gold standard in "stopping power" (that is, it makes the bad guy think twice about taking a step forward) *and* you can chamber either the .357 Magnum or the .38 Special—a lighter round, but still adequate for self-defense—in your .357 revolver. But don't be misled; you can't shoot a .357 Magnum round out of a revolver chambered for .38 Special, despite the fact that they are the same diameter (and, in fact, the .38 Special is actually .357 in diameter!)

Confused yet?

Don't feel bad. The most important lesson in ammunition is to "assume nothing." Always ask questions, read the ammo box, or take a tip from the old *Who Wants to Be a Millionaire?* game show and phone a friend.

I can't begin to count the number of people who own a standard 9mm (Luger, NATO, Parabellum, 9x19) but have purchased a box of 9mm Makarov or 9mm Largo rounds, thinking "a nine is a nine is a nine." Nope.

There are other things to consider, too. I always tell my students that the stuff you load into a magazine (or a cylinder if you have a revolver) is ammunition—or ammo or rounds or cartridges—but *not* bullets. No, I am not being a purist, and I really don't care what you call it in the privacy of your own home—and, yes, I will sometimes ask my hubby to "grab a box of bullets for my nine."

But, I stress the importance of proper terminology so you don't end up like the sheepish gentleman who came into the gun shop one day in search of a great deal on 9mm rounds. And boy he found it! At a time when Blazer Brass rounds were selling for $10.99 for fifty rounds, this

The primer cup is found in the center at the base of a center-fire round of ammo.

Ball-tip rounds, as shown above, are usually used for practice. I've shot with Blazer Brass or the less-expensive aluminum-cased ammo. If you plan to reload, always go with brass.

fellow was pretty proud of himself. He wandered to the back of the store where he triumphantly picked up a box of *one hundred* 9mm bullets for a mere $16.99. It was truly an unbeatable deal.

Until he got home and pried open the package—only to discover one hundred lumps of lead. Yep. He got bullets alright, but they don't work very well without the other three components of a cartridge—the case, the primer, and the powder. He had purchased reloading supplies rather than factory ammunition.

As the NRA basic pistol course explains, a cartridge consists of the bullet (which is the part that exits the muzzle of the gun and ultimately slams into the bad guy or the target), the case (which wraps around all the other parts to hold them together), the propellant (not gunpowder but smokeless powder these days), and, finally, the primer (which is kind of like a fuse that ignites the propellant).

So if you walk into a shop that sells reloading materials and you don't understand the mysterious ways of ammo, you may walk out with a great deal that isn't such a great deal after all.

And, yes, the gentleman who got such a steal on bullets quickly returned the box and traded it in for two boxes of 9mm cartridges.

As you continue your firearms education, you will hear the terms "centerfire" and "rimfire" bandied about. These terms refers only to the location of the primer (the fuse-like section of the cartridge).

In centerfire ammo, the primer is located in a little cup on the flat underside of the round, in, yes, the center. This is true for most of the pistol rounds you will ever shoot. The exception is the ever-popular .22 LR which is a rimfire round. That means that the primer is located at the base of the cartridge along the rim. The primer location makes this round slightly less dependable than its centerfire counterpart. This is simply because the process of roping the primer along the rim can be more problematic on an assembly line. I have run across many more .22 LR cartridges that refused to fire (probably because of insufficient primer) than I have centerfire cartridges.

So, what kind of rounds should you put in your firearm? You may have noticed that there are ball-tip rounds, +P and +P+ rounds, hollow-points, wadcutters, and so on.

Some of the answers are easy—for range shooting you will usually pick the round-nose or ball-tip ammunition, often called range rounds or practice ammo. This is typically the cheapest among the above choices. Within the ball-tip rounds, you will have aluminum-cased and brass-cased ammo. What's the difference? Well, typically the brass rounds are more costly, but if you plan to reload (that is, reuse the cases by loading them with fresh primer, propellant, and bullets) then you must have brass. Otherwise, you are free to shoot aluminum-cased rounds. I have used the Blazer brand for most of my shooting life. Blazer is owned by CCI, which also makes Federal ammunition (the whole ammo industry is pretty incestuous these days).

The only difference I've noticed between Blazer aluminum case and Blazer Brass is that the aluminum-cased ammo leaves my gun dirtier.

Gun Girl Tip #18

Ammunition is no longer safe and viable if it has been in a flood or fire or if it has been exposed to solvents or oils. If you have old or corroded ammunition, please do not toss it in the trash, nor should you take the advice of old-timers who may recommend that you bury it. The Sporting Arms and Ammunition Manufacturers' Institute (SAAMI) makes the following recommendation: "Under most circumstances, unserviceable ammunition may be scrapped by returning it to the manufacturer. Written permission should first be obtained from the Product Services Manager of the manufacturer before shipment is made." Many local hazardous waste materials disposal centers will also accept ammunition. For more information on proper use and storage of ammunition, you can download SAAMI's useful Small Arms Ammunition brochure from www.saami.org/specifications_ and_information/publications/ download/SAAMI_ITEM_202-Sporting_Ammunition.pdf

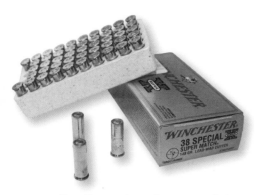

You will recognize wadcutter ammo by its distinctive flat-headed design.

Semi-wadcutter rounds are a little less severe than full wadcutters.

If you buy ammo marked as +P or +P+, make sure your gun is designed to shoot this type of ammo.

That's only an issue if you don't clean your gun regularly.

So what about all the other types of ammo I mentioned? What are they? Why are they used? And when should I use them?

WADCUTTER ROUND

These rounds are typically target rounds, due to their flat tip, which cuts a very clean hole in a paper target for scoring purposes. They have lighter recoil than standard rounds and are usually associated with revolvers because the flat end can create feeding issues in magazine-fed pistols.

SEMI-WADCUTTERS

These have the same basic function as outlined above, except that the nose of the round isn't as flat as a standard wadcutter. This makes it possible for competitive shooters to use them in semi-automatic pistols as well as revolvers.

+P

If your ammo box is marked "+P", then the rounds are a higher-pressure round than a standard ball tip. SAAMI establishes limits on what is an acceptable pressure designation for the various rounds. A typical 9mm load would have pressure in the neighborhood of 35,000 psi, while a +P round would be set to not exceed 38,500 psi. Yeah, I know—thanks for the science lesson. Now what does all that mean? It means that a

Gun Girl Tip #19

No discussion about bullets and ballistics is complete without explaining the objective of a bullet, at least in a personal defense situation. Yes, we take our ball-tip rounds out to the range on a sunny afternoon and poke holes in paper, as we should, and it's great fun. But let's get real, ladies. In the end, all that range time is a prelude to a potential nightmare scenario that involves some oversized piece of human wreckage who wants to mug, rape, or murder us (sometimes all three)—and the degree of his success will be determined by our skill and comfort with a firearm. Will we—can we—stop him with several well-placed shots to major organs? It's not pretty to think about, but neither is the horrible vision of our husband, parents, or children being forced to identify our battered and bloody corpse in some sterile, stinking morgue. Do I have your attention now? Good. So here's where I explain that there are basically three results of a handgun projectile (i.e., bullet) with regard to inflicting a wound. They are penetration, permanent cavity wound, and temporary cavity wound. Penetration means how far the projectile passes through tissue that it disturbs or destroys. Permanent cavity wound means how much of that tissue impacted by penetration is permanently destroyed—that is, how big a hole is left by the bullet. And temporary cavity wound refers to the stretching of tissue due to the kinetic energy of the bullet: many parts of the human body are surprisingly elastic, with tissue that can return to its original shape after being disrupted by a bullet. All three elements occur when you hit someone with a bullet. The secret to stopping an aggressor is to make sure that these factors conspire to (a) damage or destroy the central nervous system (through a direct hit to the head or spinal cord) or (b) strike a blood-bearing organ, thus leading to lethal blood loss. This is where many of my female students begin to cringe or look uncomfortable. We all can reach a comfort level with a handgun pretty quickly. Like anything else, practice makes perfect. But the "blood and guts" discussion about, well, blood and guts, is neither savory nor simple. But it is reality, and reality can rarely be tied up with a nice, neat bow, no matter how much we may wish it to be so.

+P round is a "hot round"—that is, it will have greater velocity than a standard round and is typically used in defensive situations, rather than for practice shooting. Is it something you want to invest in? Well, from a personal defense standpoint, it could be, but there are trade-offs. A +P round will produce greater recoil and, thus, more discomfort upon firing. It will also be harder on your gun. +P rounds are typically available in 9mm, .38 Special, and .45 ACP. Newer rounds, such as .40 S&W and .357 Sig, do not have +P versions because they were designed at a higher pressure from the start. If you feel the need to use a +P round (and I have never had that inclination), then make certain that your gun is rated for it. If it isn't, the added pressure will likely damage your barrel—if not immediately, then certainly over time. Because of the additional recoil and muzzle flip created by a higher-pressure round, I choose to avoid +P. I would rather focus on the accuracy and stability that comes with a standard round because, in the end, personal defense is more about bullet placement than the type of ammo you use.

+P+

Simply put, +P+ is an even hotter load than +P and is a round that has not been standardized by SAAMI. As a result, few guns are rated for its use. This load made its first appearance several decades ago when it was marketed by the Federal Cartridge Corporation in a 9mm caliber and labeled "For Law Enforcement Only"—which, of course, ensured that it would become a prized possession for all those who wanted to be as cool as the cops (or as lethal). I get mixed reviews on its value, and, if you scan the internet for +P+ articles and comments, you will get a similar array of opinions. For beginners, I would steer clear for now and just get comfortable practicing with your ball-tip rounds or using the tried-and-true hollow-points and/or polymer-tipped cartridges for personal defense.

HOLLOW-POINTS

I have been fascinated by hollow-points since I began shooting, and my interest extended to wading through the 1989 FBI report *Handgun Wounding Factors and Effectiveness*. The report is available on the internet and is a treasure trove of information regarding ballistics and handgun effectiveness. The report first confirms what every cop friend has ever told me: that the best personal defense weapon is *not* a handgun or, more colorfully, "I just carry a pistol so I can fend off the bastards long enough to get to my shotgun."

But the report also acknowledges that, like it or not, handguns are the primary defensive weapon in an unexpected attack—and this applies to both law enforcement and to us average joes with concealed carry permits. (Anyway, it is pretty tough to conceal and carry a shotgun—or even one of today's popular pistols that are chambered for .410 shotgun shells.)

The FBI further acknowledged that, regardless of how many rounds their magazines held—and some models today, such as the Springfield XD(M), hold up to nineteen rounds—most law enforcement officers engaged in a firefight were lucky to get one or two rounds into the aggressor's torso. Think about that for a moment—we're talking about professional lawmen with years of range practice and ample experience dealing with "the fog of war." And only one or two rounds that actually hit the mark? Yikes. How much worse might those poor schmucks shoot who have never fired a gun in self-defense—and who visit the range twice a year for forty-five minutes of practice?

An assortment of hollow-points, the traditional style and the polymer-tipped models.

And, thus, the FBI concludes that pistols are an imperfect solution to an imperfect world, and it is all the more important to select ammo that will maximize the impact of your impact! In other words, the name of the game is making the biggest possible hole in the bad guy's body so he will, at a minimum, decide you are not worth the effort—and, at a maximum, never be able to accost anyone again. And so we come to the much-vaunted and often-maligned hollow-point bullet.

The mushroom effect that occurs when a hollow-point strikes something.

The purpose of a hollow-point is to maximize the impact of your shot by doing the most possible damage to the tissue. Sound cruel? Actually, no, because a hollow-point also minimizes the likelihood that the bullet will pass through your intended target and into an innocent bystander.

Whereas a ball-tipped cartridge is topped by a solid, round (or blunt in the case of a .40 S&W) projectile, the hollow-point's projectile is open at the tip. This design causes the bullet to mushroom upon impact, which, in turn, stops the bullet's forward momentum, and, in the process, increases the size of the permanent cavity created during penetration. In the end, the degree of penetration and permanent cavity (not to mention the placement of the bullet) will determine whether your assailant is disabled by your shots.

The hollow-points of yesteryear were effective in creating a sizeable permanent cavity (when they actually mushroomed) but not so effective in penetrating. As a result, you will still run into old-timers who argue heatedly against the use of hollow-points. Even the 1989 FBI report points out that hollow-points of the late twentieth century only managed to expand effectively 60 to 70 percent of the time, and that their expansion—the whole point of having a hollow-point—often impeded the bullet's ability to penetrate very deeply. The result would be a gaping, but ineffective, flesh wound!

What's the value of a round that doesn't penetrate well when it expands—and doesn't create the desired wound severity when it doesn't expand? Penetration *and* permanent cavity are necessary to effectively fell an attacker (with penetration being the more important of the two).

There are a variety of good personal defense rounds out there. Do your research and pick the one you prefer. Pictured above are Hornady Critical Defense, Federal Hydra-Shok, and Speer Gold Dot.

To this day, the online firearms and ammo discussion groups debate and belabor the effectiveness of hollow-points. But much has changed in the past twenty-five years. Modern hollow-point expansion is much more reliable, and many manufacturers claim up to a 95 percent "provable" expansion rate. The 1989 FBI report also addressed the issue of the hollow tips filling up with fibers from clothing, which would impede the bullet's ability to expand (causing it to behave like a standard round-nose bullet). This phenomenon was compounded by the low muzzle velocity of handgun rounds. Likewise, the report faulted hollow-point expansion with limiting the penetration of the round. Modern ammunition manufacturers have struggled to remedy both these issues, or, more accurately, to strike a balance between the two, and have achieved a measure of success (although no ammunition can claim 100 percent reliability). Features such as crimped edges and polymer tips have improved both penetration and expansion. I have read numerous test results from a variety of reputable sources that tested modern rounds on 10 percent ordnance gelatin, leather, material, and even wood, and I have been impressed by the results—impressed enough to feel confident with modern hollow-points in my carry gun.

I am personally a fan of Hornady's Critical Defense and Critical Duty rounds (with their strange little polymer tips that look like someone

Gun Girl Tip #20

If you decide to carry hollow-points, I recommend you swallow hard and purchase a twenty-five-round pack explicitly for range shooting. Yes, they cost more and you certainly don't want to use them as range rounds on a regular basis, but you *do* want to see how they perform in your firearm. Some guns can be finicky about feeding hollow-points. I have heard this dismissed as a myth or attributed to the old military-issue 1911s of yesteryear, but I have seen it in modern-day firearms and, in fact, experienced it with my very new and very expensive Sig Sauer 1911. It did not want to feed open-tipped hollow-points but fed polymer-tipped hollow-points with no trouble. Likewise, we have had customers with other types of handguns who have reported feeding issues. Unusual? Perhaps. But I'd just as soon find out on the range as in the midst of a personal defense encounter.

shoved an eraser into the opening). My law enforcement hubby favors Speer Gold Dot and Federal Hydra-Shok. We could argue all day long about which brand is superior, but it is clear that modern hollow-points have overcome many of the early issues cited by the FBI.

Another tidbit of knowledge about ammunition: when you pick up a box of ammo and see that it lists a certain number of grains per round, that has nothing to do with grains of gunpowder. It is a measurement of the weight of the bullet itself (the projectile, versus the entire piece of ammunition). So, in 9mm for instance, 115 gr would be a lighter bullet, 124 a little heavier, and 147 even heavier.

And, as I touched on in chapter 3, please walk away from anyone who urges you to select a particular caliber based on its "knockdown power." A handgun round does not have the power to knock someone off their feet. Period. But, that having been said, people *do* often fall down when they have been shot. Why? Because television and films have conditioned them to believe they should. The FBI report concluded that people fall down when shot because they see people on television fall down when they are shot. It's as simple as that. But don't purchase a particular caliber of gun for its ability to drop someone, because you may be very disappointed at a quite inopportune time.

Similarly, "stopping power" is a term that can be misleading. The whole idea of using a firearm in self-defense is to *stop* someone from hurting you or a loved one. But how quickly you actually stop them depends on many factors, some of which you will have no control over. Unless you score a head or heart shot, your assailant may not even know he's been hit. And even if he realizes it, the human body has the ability to continue functioning long after parts have been compromised by the impact of a bullet. When a body is in fight-or-flight mode, it is capable of much greater feats of strength and endurance than after it recovers from its adrenaline high. I still recall a scene from the film *The Untouchables* where a bullet-riddled Sean Connery painfully drags himself off a fire escape and down the main hallway of his house in order to leave a clue for Elliot Ness (Kevin Costner). Although I loved the movie, this scene always seemed ridiculous to me—until I began to read more about ballistics and the impact of bullets on human flesh. It is, in fact, probably more realistic than many of the nightly crime dramas or the old time Westerns where one or two rounds send the bad guy crashing through a plate-glass window.

The durability of the human body is also an argument against limiting the number of rounds available in a pistol—and the biggest reason why

I am not a revolver fan. I want as *many rounds* at my disposal as possible, since I will likely have to shoot many times in order to (a) hit what I am shooting at and (b) convince my target that he would be well-advised to abandon his pursuit.

This is why I am endlessly frustrated by media pundits who second-guess the police with such inane questions as "Why didn't he shoot to wound?" or "Why did he need to shoot the guy so many times—isn't that overkill?" And those are direct quotes, "ripped from the headlines" as the media like to say.

Why? Well, because (a) a wounded person can still kill you or others and (b) put yourself into a gunfight and tell me you won't use every available round to disable or dissuade your attacker.

I was especially dismayed when Vice President Joe Biden advised that women should have a double-barrel shotgun in their homes and should "fire two blasts outside the house" when threatened by an intruder. Uh—what?

The only part of the equation he got right was the presence of a shotgun. But you'd be a darned sight better off with a Kel-Tec KSG (which holds thirteen rounds) than with a traditional double-barrel model. And why in the heck would you waste two rounds firing "outside the house"? Why not greet the intruder in the hallway and use those two rounds on him? It's advice like this that makes me wonder if some of our elected officials are closet misogynists. What else could explain advising a woman to frivolously expend her only means of defense when under attack? It boggles the mind.

AMMO MALFUNCTIONS

As a novice shooter, you should stick with store-bought ammunition versus trying your hand at reloading or snagging a great deal on military surplus ammo. My pal Buddy is the consummate salesman—always on the hunt for a great deal, always looking for a way around paying retail. And those deals have included purchasing sealed cans of foreign military munitions that were buried in the sand after World War II and dug up a few years ago for resale.

"Hey, they've been hermetically sealed in herring cans," Buddy explains. "They're as good as the day they were manufactured."

Well, maybe—but manufacturing standards have changed dramatically since 1946, and I would rather pay a little more and know that my ammunition was produced by a company that still exists and would be liable for any imperfections or malfunctions.

And factory ammunition does malfunction from time to time, but such issues are few and far between.

In the NRA's basic pistol class, we educate students about four types of malfunctions: the misfire, the hangfire, the squib load, and the stovepipe. In over a decade of pistol shooting, I have seen a few misfires (usually with .22s), few if any squib loads, no hangfires that I could discern, and a whole bunch of stovepipes, mainly because this malfunction is typically user-induced!

A misfire occurs when, for whatever reason, the round simply doesn't light. Either the primer is missing or insufficient or there is a problem with the propellant inside the cartridge. For whatever reason, the round simply doesn't fire, although the gun itself is functioning properly. And so you are left holding an active yet inactive firearm, not sure what to do next. First of all, above all else, keep that gun pointed downrange (that is, toward the targets). I will never forget being in an instructor class with an awkward gent who seemed ill-equipped for gun handling. He had trouble grasping the lessons and also had issues controlling the recoil and muzzle flip on his .357 Magnum revolver. While I believe no one has the right to tell you that you may not own a handgun (unless you are a felon or have committed a domestic violence offense), I do concede that there are some folks who should probably find a less lethal tool for personal defense. He may have been one of them.

At one point during our range time, he pulled his trigger and nothing happened. Instead of following the protocol of keeping the gun pointed downrange while raising his non-dominant hand so the instructor could assist him, he turned toward the group behind him, gun leveled straight at us, finger on the trigger, sweeping our entire group, including our seventy-five-year-old master NRA instructor, Ed Danielewicz, who sprung forward with the agility of an eighteen-year-old to relieve him of his firearm. I had never before seen Ed angry, but I thought he was going to punch the little guy in the nose. "You *never* do that. *Ever*," he told the flustered student. "If your gun doesn't fire *you stay right where you are and let me come to you*." Couldn't have said it better myself.

Thankfully, the guy truly had a misfire. If he'd been holding a hangfire, life would have changed dramatically for someone! A hangfire happens when detonation of the primer and/or powder is delayed. That doesn't mean minutes, just seconds. But seconds can feel like minutes when you are holding a gun. A hangfire can delay for up to thirty seconds, and, thus, you don't want to be pointing the gun at anyone or staring into the muzzle pondering the problem. Once again, if you are on the range, raise your hand and wait for a range officer; then, with the gun still pointed downrange, explain the situation. If you're by yourself, wait a minute or so, to be certain it is a misfire, and then rack open the slide (muzzle still pointed downrange) and eject the dud cartridge. If the blame lies with faulty ammo, you should be able to resume shooting as the new round moves into the chamber. If it still doesn't fire, repeat the waiting sequence and then drop the magazine and eject the cartridge. At this point, I would recommend seeking guidance from someone with gun knowledge; it's pretty unlikely that you would have two duds in a row. You might also retrieve the two ejected rounds and take them to your gun guru. If you see a small dent in the primer cup, then the problem may be a light strike; that is, the firing pin or hammer is not hitting the primer cup hard enough to detonate it.

If a misfire or hangfire occurs with a revolver versus a semi-automatic, you will simply wait thirty to sixty seconds before pulling the trigger again and cycling the cylinder to the next round. This is one of the advantages of a wheel gun!

When I think about the manufacturing process, I marvel that more factory rounds aren't defective, but it is rare to have either a misfire (from faulty ammo) or a hangfire. And when I have had one, it is almost always with .22 LR ammo, likely because of the more delicate process of feeding the primer around the rim.

The next potential glitch in your shooting experience is a defect known as a squib load. A squib occurs when the cartridge lacks sufficient propellant (smokeless powder) to send it as far downrange as it would normally go. A squib is only a problem if the force is so weak that the bullet doesn't even clear the muzzle.

Squib loads are the reason most ranges prohibit rapid-fire exercises. If your first round is a squib that fails to exit the barrel and you quickly stack up three or four more rounds right behind it, then you've got a problem. I've seen barrels that were split open or even peeled back like a banana by the force of a secondary round crashing into a squib load. The best one was a six-inch barrel that Master Instructor Ed brought to class one day. It boasted three or four large bulges, looking for all the world like a python that had devoured a family of mice.

I've never encountered a squib that failed to exit the barrel, although I have had one or two rounds that seemed to lack the appropriate sound and force, which is how it is with most squibs. In fact, if you always use factory ammo and avoid reloads, you may never encounter a squib load.

But no matter what quality ammo you use, if you shoot a semi-automatic handgun, you will undoubtedly eventually find yourself staring at a stovepipe—probably more than one. Stovepipes look just as their

A stovepipe is so named because it looks like, well, a stovepipe.

name implies—like a tiny chimney peeking through the ejection port. They occur when the slide fails to cycle with enough energy to expel the spent casing, and it gets trapped in mid ejection. The culprit is almost always the shooter—something she didn't do (like clean or oil the gun) or something she did do (like limp-wrist the recoil).

Over the years, I have developed the ability to watch a shooter and predict the probability of stovepiping. When you see those wrists flying back with every shot, you can pretty much count on the inevitability of a stovepipe! Weak wrists interrupt the inertia of the slide, not allowing it to complete its cycle, and, suddenly, the whole shooting sequence grinds to a screeching halt. The short-term cure is to keep the gun pointed in a safe direction (finger off the trigger, of course), remove the magazine, and then turn the gun upside down (ejection port facing the ground) and pull back on the slide, shaking the weapon so the casing falls free.

This will allow you to resume shooting, but it won't guarantee that you won't stovepipe again minutes later. If this malfunction is caused by your grip, then you will have to work harder to keep those wrists locked and prevent the gun from firing you instead of the reverse. Chapter 8 will help you understand how to overcome grip and stance issues, but your problem may be that the gun you have chosen is simply too powerful for your particular body type. You may be better served by finding a different firearm.

Gun Girl Tip #21

The best ammo in the world is useless if you don't know how to load it into your gun. Loading a revolver is easy: hold the gun with the muzzle pointed at the ground, swing open the cylinder, and drop your rounds into the individual chambers. Latch the cylinder back into the frame and away you go! But I routinely watch students break into a cold sweat as they attempt to stuff rounds into a magazine. It can be hard on the thumbs, and it is made worse by an irrational fear that the rounds will "go off" if not treated with kid gloves. Stop worrying! Modern ammo is held to strict control measures that keep it extremely safe. Take the magazine in your non-dominant hand and pick up a round of ammo in your dominant hand. Then use the butt of the cartridge to press down on the follower, and, in so doing, slide the round under the lips or shoulders of the magazine, so it stays in place and is forced upward by the follower. There are "magazine loaders" available, and many modern double-stack firearms actually come with one. But before you take shortcuts, make sure you can load the old-fashioned way. Otherwise, if you have to load a magazine quickly—and there is no mag loader close at hand—you could be in a world of hurt.

Then again, you may not be the issue—at least not directly. If you don't clean your weapon regularly or if you are one of those folks who thinks that a drop of oil on the slide rails is sufficient, then your stovepiping may be easily cured: clean and lube your gun!

Once you have successfully loaded your ammo, what exactly happens when you pull that trigger? It's really pretty simple, and all parts of the cartridge play a role. As soon as that hammer or firing pin falls forward and strikes the primer cup (or the rim, on .22 LR ammo), the primer ignites and begins to burn the powder or propellant inside the cartridge. As the powder burns, it generates hot gasses (I like to call this the "taco effect") which build up pressure in the chamber. As heat and pressure build, the metal case expands, creating a seal that prevents the gas from escaping to the rear. As pressure continues to build, the bullet is forced out of the now-loosened metal case and speeds down the bore, propelled by the expanding gas. When the bullet breaks free of the muzzle and all those hot gasses hit the atmosphere, a loud noise ensues, not unlike the ultimate result of eating one too many tacos! (Okay—well, my students think that's funny.)

CHAPTER SUMMARY

- Don't expect the American system of naming ammunition to make any sense. Why? Because there is no American system for naming ammunition!

- Europeans identify their ammunition in millimeters—diameter x length: 9x19, etc.

- You can fire .38 Special rounds out of a gun chambered for .357 Magnum. You cannot do the reverse.

- A bullet is not the same thing as ammunition. A bullet is just one part of a four-piece ammunition cartridge, which consists of primer, propellant, case, and bullet.

- Centerfire cartridges have the primer located in a little cup at the base of the round (in the center, of course). On a rimfire cartridge, the primer is located around the rim of the base.

- There are a variety of different styles of ammo, ranging from wadcutter and semi-wadcutter to +P and hollow-points. Each has a use that ranges from target shooting to personal defense. Make sure the ammo you select is right for your gun and for your purpose—that is, it is costly and wasteful to send expensive hollow-points downrange for practice when standard-practice (ball-tip) rounds would do.

- Bullets do not make people fall down. People fall down when shot because they have been conditioned by Hollywood to believe they should. "Knockdown power" is a myth.

- Actually stopping someone with a bullet is all about bullet placement. Only a direct heart or head shot will stop someone in their tracks. In a self-defense situation, you will not only likely have to fire many shots, but you will also probably only hit your intended target a couple times. When it comes to ammo in a self-defense scenario, more is better!

- Ammunition malfunctions in modern factory ammo are very, very rare. Probably the worst you will encounter is a stovepipe, which is typically your fault anyway. Proper grip and proper maintenance will lessen or prevent stovepipes.

CHAPTER 8

ON THE RANGE

So now you are well-versed in the fundamentals of revolvers, semi-autos, and ballistics. You know the differences between them and perhaps even which model will work best for you. Along the way, you have, hopefully, taken some advice from folks with experience—and *ignored* some advice from folks with experience (and from folks who don't know what the heck they're talking about, but want to get their two cents worth in anyway!).

Perhaps you have purchased the gun of your dreams (for now—there will be another, I guarantee it). Or maybe you are borrowing a friend's gun to get in a little range time.

If you have taken an NRA basic pistol course, then your head has been filled with more information than you will ever retain in one sitting, and you are probably worrying about all the things you have to remember when you step up to the firing line.

Believe me, I recall that sinking feeling when you fear that your brain just isn't large enough to hold all the knowledge necessary to own and operate a gun. I had the same feeling the day I took my first driver's ed class when I was sixteen. I couldn't imagine that I would ever remember to do all the things that seemed to be simultaneously required of me in order to drive—and drive safely.

Similarly, I have a vivid recollection of driving away from the hospital with my newborn son in my arms thinking, "Are these people crazy? They just let me walk out with this baby. I have no idea what to do with it! I'll probably break it or lose it or something. There's no way I'll ever be able to learn everything I need to know to keep one of these!"

Well, I have managed to successfully drive a car for the past thirty-five years, and my son made it through twenty-one years with only a few bumps, bruises, and contusions—most of them self-induced. And, yes, my

Gun Girl Tip #22

One of the dangers you may face during your range time has nothing to do with the gun you are shooting. If you are female, be prepared for periodic unwanted advice from well-meaning and not-so-well-meaning male shooters. The intrusions can range from mildly distracting to wildly inappropriate. You do not have to put up with this, and you need to make that clear to range management. In response to male intrusions, I have smiled politely and said, "Thank you but I need to work on this myself." I have also complained to range management when one of the range safety officers (RSOs) persisted in approaching me in my range lane and offering advice and comment. He went so far as to take the gun out of my hand in order to share his gun wisdom with me. Now, mind you, I was not violating any range rules; I was simply practicing shooting techniques and his "advice" was essentially unrelated to my shooting—much more an effort to show off than to improve my shooting style. But, even if his guidance had been useful, it was nonetheless unsolicited. The RSO is there to keep people safe. Period. If you have a problem, he is there to help. And, yes, if you have a question, by all means speak up. But he is not there to instruct.

Likewise, if anyone tries to tinker with your gun—adjusting the sights, for instance—don't let it happen. Most modern pistol sights are factory set, and before you let a novice, or even an experienced shooter, tamper with them, make certain the problem is the sights and not the shooter. In my early days of shooting, I had a nosey gentleman at a local range adjust my P22 sights so far out of whack that I had to pay money to get them back to factory specs. I was a beginner and very uncertain of range etiquette. I didn't want to look like an overly defensive female, so I let this gentleman modify my gun. Thankfully, my friend Mike was shooting in the next lane and interceded to prevent any additional damage to the gun. I am amazed by the liberties a man will take on the range with a female shooter—liberties he would never dream of taking with another man (for obvious reasons).

It's not something you should live in fear of—but be aware. On the flip side, however, you should never hesitate to seek guidance from those with more skill and experience—and, frankly, that will usually be a man. Most of what I know about firearms, I learned from men, but I will choose my own experts, thank you. It isn't a sign of weakness to ask questions. Just make sure you are asking them of someone with the wisdom and maturity to offer actual answers versus a sleazy attempt at a come-on.

initial fear of guns and of whether I could retain the knowledge necessary to use them safely has also faded with time and experience.

So ladies, if you have mastered child rearing, driving, cooking, running a business, or anything else that once seemed daunting, I have no doubt that learning to use a firearm safely and competently will come just as easily.

So now you have a gun, whether it is one you have purchased or one you are borrowing from a friend to try out. You want to venture out to the range but you are concerned about looking incompetent and being safe. Trust me—everyone who has ever hoisted a firearm has had those same fears (at least everyone with any sense!).

My first recommendation, before you ever fire that first round and certainly before you slap down a bundle on a handgun, is that you spend some time in the NRA's basic pistol class (or a similar class offered by reputable organizations such as the National Shooting Sports Foundation or the US Concealed Carry Association) and also take whatever training is necessary in your state to secure a concealed carry permit (bearing in mind that such a permit is easier to secure in some states than in others). You might also track down a local class on firearms and the law. I don't agree with all the gun laws on the books, but I am careful to abide by them. While I may advocate on behalf of rolling back certain pieces of gun legislation, it doesn't change the fact that I am a law-abiding citizen, and I would rather work to change the system from within than confirm the worst accusations of the anti-gun lobby by operating outside the law.

So, what does that mean? That means, at a minimum, know the laws of your state and abide by them with regard to using and transporting a firearm. If you cannot find, or don't wish to attend, a class on guns and the law, then reference the state-by-state list in the back of this book, or look up your state attorney general's web site for a quick primer on the gun laws in your state.

In Ohio, for instance, if you don't have a concealed carry permit and you are driving to the range with your gun, you must make sure the gun is in the trunk and the ammo in the glove box, or vice versa. The law requires that you should not be able to combine the two without exiting your car.

Once you have a concealed carry permit, you should sign up for legislative updates in order to be certain that you always know the laws of your state and nation. Ignorance is not a defense.

So once you have made it safely to the range and not broken any laws in the process, it is finally time to step up to the firing line and take those first shots. Hopefully, you have a gun with you that fits your hand

and is reasonably comfortable to shoot. Before you begin poking holes in paper, make sure you ask the range management for a copy of the SOP—standard operating procedures. Every range has a set of rules that you are expected to know and abide by. Take the time to familiarize yourself with those rules to avoid being corrected by the range safety officer, or, worse yet, thrown off the range altogether. You will also likely have to sign a waiver absolving the range of any responsibility should something go terribly wrong. Don't freak out—it is standard lawyer stuff that you have to sign almost anytime you do anything that involves a modicum of risk.

Barring any unwanted attentions from fellow shooters, you can find your shooting lane and begin organizing your range supplies. Most ranges require that you keep the breech of your gun open (that is, the slide locked back) when you are not shooting, so, as soon as you pull out your gun, lock it back, or, in the case of a revolver, swing the empty cylinder out.

You will also be required to wear both hearing and eye protection. If you wear glasses, it is not necessary to fit the eye protection over your glasses; your prescription lenses are adequate coverage. The purpose of eye protection is to prevent spent casings, hot debris, etc. from flying into your eyes. Your regular glasses can do that as well as the plastic safety goggles. And be aware that there are eye doctors who specialize in shooting glasses, so if you want the protection of the larger goggles with the benefit of your own prescription, you can plop down a little cash and get the best of both worlds.

I prefer the flanged Howard Leight earplugs because they fit down into my ear canal. This gives me better noise attenuation . . . and doesn't mess up my hair!

One quick note for those of us who have progressed into the wonderful world of bi- and trifocal glasses: You can shoot with your prescription lenses, but make certain that you select a section of the glasses to look through and do not deviate. It is not unusual to discover that a really bad shooter has been alternating between high and low on her bifocals. Pick a spot and stick with it or your shots will be scattered all over the target.

Hearing protection is another subjective choice. I prefer the foam or soft plastic pieces that actually fit into my ears. Part of it is vanity—I hate to wear things that mash my hair—and part of it is that they seem to block the sound better than many of the muff-style protectors I've worn. That having been said, I hear great things about the noise-attenuating earmuffs, such as those produced by the Howard Leight company. Leight also makes my favorite plugs, the AirSoft brand, with flexible flanges that fit snugly in my ear canal. For my money, these are superior to the foam plugs that seem to pop out at inopportune times.

I will eventually invest in a set of the noise-attenuating muffs. As I age (ugh) and my hearing deteriorates, I find it almost impossible to teach a range class without popping my plugs in and out constantly. The Leight muffs (and others like them) actually allow you to hear voices clearly while filtering out background noise and, of course, the sharp crack of gunfire. Hearing will ultimately win out over vanity for me, and that's okay.

Eye and ear protection are essential on the range to make the most of your shooting experience.

Assuming you have purchased or borrowed eyewear and ear protection, you are ready to focus on what the NRA calls "The Fundamentals of Pistol Shooting." These include your hand-eye dominance, your grip, aiming, trigger control, shooting position, and more. They are all important to know, but experience has taught me that a couple elements are vastly more critical to a successful shoot.

Using your hands and eyes properly is high on the list of must-dos. You probably already know whether you are right-handed or left-handed, but you may not know whether you are right-eye dominant or left-eye dominant. In order to find out, you can perform this simple exercise with your hands:

Straighten both arms in front of you with palms facing outward and the tips of your index fingers meeting, while your thumbs overlap,

This simple exercise will help you determine whether your dominant eye and hand match.

creating a little triangle with your hands. Keeping your arms extended and your hands together as shown, pick an object in the room, like a light switch or doorknob, and place it in the center of your little hand triangle. Now close your right eye. Is the object still centered in the triangle? If so, then you are left-eye dominant. But if you are now staring at the back of your hand instead of the object, then you are right-eye dominant. To be sure, close your left eye. Whichever eye is open when you can still see the object centered in the triangle, that is your dominant eye. If you can't get your hands positioned correctly (and I have students in every class that struggle with this), then grab a CD or DVD and hold it at arm's length, placing your chosen object in the middle of the hole. Do the same blinking exercise, and you'll get your answer.

More than likely, if you are right-handed, you will be right-eye dominant and vice versa. But that isn't always true—and, in most classes, I usually have at least one student who is cross dominant, that is, right-handed but left-eye dominant or left-handed and right-eye dominant. Since you aim with your dominant eye, it is pretty important to know which eye will be doing the work.

If you're dominant hand and eye line up, good for you. You'll simply look through the sights and find your target. But if you are cross dominant, aiming can become an exercise in contorting your head down to your shoulder so that your left eye lines up with your right arm or the reverse. You definitely don't want to shoot that way, even if you could find a way to do it comfortably. The good news is that it is easier for pistol shooters to accommodate cross dominance than it is for those who shoot long guns (rifles and shotguns). You can't change the dominance that's hardwired into your body, but you can accommodate it or compensate for it in one of several ways.

I preface this section by saying that I am not cross dominant; I only know what I have been taught about it and how my cross-dominant friends have compensated for it. If one of these solutions fails to address the problem, then progress to the next one.

1. **Simply move the gun over a couple inches so it is in front of your dominant eye.** Huh? Well, that was certainly easy. I recently had a concealed carry student who was cross dominant and had had her gun sights adjusted to (supposedly) accommodate her cross dominance. The only problem was that when she hit the firing line, her pattern was terrible. After unsuccessfully using the standard techniques to try to correct it, I dug out my own gun of the same make and model and handed it to her, instructing her to simply line it up with her dominant eye and shoot. Wonder of wonders, her pattern and confidence improved dramatically!

2. **If solution #1 doesn't work for you, you can always try controlling the firearm with your non-dominant hand.** This will allow you to aim with your dominant eye. However, if you are like me, the concentration power required to go from a right-handed grip to a left-handed grip (or vice versa) is almost prohibitive. But, interestingly, the students I have had who are cross dominant seem to have a much easier time switching between hands. Apparently, nature has compensated for the challenges of being cross dominant.

3. **Close your dominant eye and learn to target with your non-dominant eye.** It will feel strange at first but it can be done. Some shooters even don an eye patch so there is no temptation to use the dominant eye.

4. **Finally, if all else fails, you can try having your sights adjusted to compensate for the cross dominance,** remembering the cautionary tale I told in solution #1. Do not attempt to do this yourself. Find a good gunsmith who has made successful sight alterations in the past. Let him do the dirty work so you don't end up with a useless firearm.

GRIP

My trips to the range were all pretty frustrating until I perfected my grip and stance. And, of those two, proper grip had the greatest impact. If you are old enough to have watched television in the 1970s, you probably learned to "teacup" a gun—basically hold it in your dominant hand while resting the butt of the grip in your cupped non-dominant hand. I am forever adjusting the fingers and thumbs of older beginners who have no practical shooting experience beyond watching *Charlie's Angels* or *The Streets of San Francisco*. The problem with the teacup hold is that you surrender much of your control over the muzzle flip and recoil.

The old "teacup" hold is seriously impractical, causing you to give up half your control of the firearm. Many people—including those in the military—were trained this way, but it is no longer viable.

Almost as common as the teacup hold is the "thumb on either side" grip, which is often followed quickly by the "thumb ripped open and bleeding" stance. If all you remember initially is that *both thumbs go on the same side of the gun*, you will be spared the agony of "slide bite," which happens when part of your hand—usually the tender web of your thumb—is sitting high enough at the back of the gun that the sharp rails of the fast-moving slide slice through it as the gun cycles the next round. I've seen some pretty grisly examples of slide bite, but proper grip will prevent it completely. I've heard it said that "everyone gets slide bite sooner or later." Well, so far, I have avoided it, though I have managed to catch the tender flesh of my palm in the ejection port more than once.

Putting one thumb on either side of the slide is a prescription for a nasty case of slide bite. Both thumbs always go on the *same* side—dominant thumb atop non-dominant.

I attribute my absence of slide bite to the fact that I rarely vary my grip, because I shoot so much better when I hold the gun properly!

Your dominant thumb lies atop the non-dominant thumb. Whether your thumbs point upward or forward is immaterial; the motion of the slide will not hurt your thumbs.

Note that your non-dominant thumb just rests beneath the dominant thumb. Don't try to tuck it into the trigger guard; just let it rest near or along the frame.

And what is the proper grip? Well, the photo shows you. Getting the hang of this grip can be a challenge. It will feel awkward at first, but the more you use it, the more it becomes second nature. I couldn't hold my pistols any other way now, despite feeling initially awkward as I fired.

Acquiring this grip requires some initial thought and effort. If you have a modern polymer-framed gun, take a look at the upper part of the grip, near the slide. You will likely note an indentation in the grip. This is where you put your thumb—not the digit itself but the fleshly part at the base of your non-dominant hand. That seems to be the hardest thing for people to grasp. I am always prying thumbs loose and repositioning them. Your actual non-dominant thumb (the digit itself) doesn't go anywhere specific. It just rests along the frame beside the trigger (many people try to tuck it into the trigger guard—not a good idea). It provides the platform that your dominant thumb lies on top of.

Foot position on the Weaver Stance places one foot (non-dominant) slightly in front of the other, much like a boxer stands.

Your dominant hand will wrap around the front strap, with your non-dominant fingers wrapped over them. Of course, your trigger finger will lie along the frame until such a time as you are ready to begin shooting. Yes, this grip feels awkward at first but it grows on you. More important, it maximizes your control of the firearm, especially when combined with a good stance.

You want to grip the gun firmly (without leaving waffle marks on your palms), and you will also want to be sure to lock your wrists. Keeping your arms properly extended in front of you will lock your wrists, but it sometimes takes a while to understand what works and what doesn't.

STANCE

As with grips, stances go in and out of style and, frankly, if you are shooting well on the range, I don't go too crazy on your stance, as long as you look comfortable. But your stance is the platform on which your shooting style is built, and it can mean the difference between life and death in a tactical situation.

When I began teaching concealed carry classes, we advocated in favor of one stance—now, conventional wisdom and law enforcement input has instructors advocating in favor of a different one. Preferences change with research, experience, and individual situations. And many of these preferences are dictated more by extreme tactical situations, such as those encountered by the police, than by simple range shooting or even personal and home defense (where you will likely not even be thinking about a stance and may be in a position you never anticipated, such as cowering in a closet or crouched behind a bed).

My NRA master instructor made a great case for what is called the "Weaver stance." He showed us how foot placement in the stance created

The Weaver stance features bent elbows and isometric tension to help control the muzzle flip.

more stability, making it harder to knock the shooter backward. He also stressed that recoil is minimized by the stance's emphasis on pulling slightly backward with the non-dominant hand while pushing forward with the dominant hand.

The Weaver stance was developed by Deputy Sheriff Jack Weaver and popularized by gun guru the late Col. Jeff Cooper in his books and training classes. Using the grip we have previously discussed, the elbow of your dominant arm is slightly bent while the supporting arm's elbow is bent downward. The shooter presses forward with his/her dominant hand while pulling backward slightly with the support hand, creating an isometric tension that helps to control muzzle flip, thus allowing for faster follow-up shots.

The second element of the stance involves placing your feet in a boxer's stance, with your non-dominant foot out front of the dominant foot. Imagine yourself boxing—you'll swing out with your dominant arm while placing your weight on your non-dominant foot, which has a balancing effect. The knee on the outward leg is "soft" or slightly bent, while the dominant leg is almost straight and slightly to the back. It is indeed a very stable platform and I shot that way for years, until my law enforcement hubby told me that the Weaver had gone out of favor with the LEOs (law enforcement officers), who were now training in the Isosceles stance because of the ease of movement from that stance.

Recently, my husband and I trained a group of students, several of whom were already comfortable with the Weaver stance. When the time came for moving and shooting, these ladies had to completely readjust their stances in order to step off effectively, moving forward and backward. They had to fall back on the Isoceles stance, which requires you to face the target squarely, with your feet shoulder width apart and your knees soft or slightly bent. The handgun is extended in front of you, with your arms straight and your wrists locked. Your shoulders are squared so your arms form an isosceles triangle (a triangle that has two sides of equal length), just as your legs do. The Isoceles is also much easier to remember in a high-stress situation. Although, again, your focus in a personal defense encounter should not be on form but on bullet placement.

Determining the stance that is best for you will come with trial and error. I would recommend starting out with the Isoceles and eventually getting into some moving and shooting classes so that you can understand the importance of being able to step out of your stance.

The Isoceles stance, pictured above, offers a very stable platform from which you can easily step off in order to move and shoot.

However, there is validity in trying every stance and being certain you can shoot effectively that way. It is also important to learn to shoot effectively with one hand—both right and left. If one hand is injured, you must be able to effectively defend yourself with the other. It sounds like a creepy nightmare scenario—and it is—but we spend an awful lot of time learning pointless skills in this life. How about spending a few minutes of every shooting session trying some skills that may eventually save your life?

WHAT TO KNOW—AND WHAT TO DO

Once you know your proper grip and stance, you are ready to begin live fire. Most indoor ranges have a place for coats and range bags, and then a counter or bench across the actual shooting lane where you set your gun and your ammunition. This also provides a convenient barrier that you should never step beyond during live fire. As with any shooting situation, range officials will expect you to keep the gun pointed in a safe direction and keep your finger off the trigger until you are ready to begin firing. As noted earlier, they will also expect you to ask for and familiarize yourself with their range rules. Make sure that the gun you pull from your range bag and carry to the lane bench is completely empty, magazine out, and slide locked back. Carry your box of ammo separately to the shooting lane and load it there, keeping the muzzle pointed downrange at all times. And when you set your gun down on the bench, set it down with the slide locked back and the ejection port face up—or, if you are using a revolver, the cylinder open.

This all sounds pretty nitpicky doesn't it? Well, if you've ever been reprimanded by an RSO (and most new shooters have been at some point), then you know why it is something to avoid. But you have to look at it from the RSO's perspective—he has a job where one mistake could get him, or someone else, killed. And I have seen people do some stupid things on the range, so I try to cut the RSOs plenty of slack. On the other hand, you will occasionally find an RSO who is a complete range Nazi, and the best you can do is steer clear, obey every rule to the letter, and, if the RSO's demands are unreasonable, complain to management (or find a new place to shoot). I have done all of the above, from time to time.

Most indoor ranges today are mechanized, and you'll need to ask

Gun Girl Tip #23

In recent years, I have advised my students to utilize elements of both stances. Shooting success comes most readily when students use the foot and body position of the Isosceles stance but apply the isometric tension common to the Weaver stance. The Weaver's push-pull force often minimizes a new shooter's tendency to press the barrel downward to compensate for recoil. This flinching habit is why so many new shooters tend to shoot low at first. Much to my pleasure, I recently read an article explaining that this blending of the two stances is the newest rage in tactical training.

for a briefing on how to move the targets forward and back. You'll also need to buy your target and get a target backing (a piece of cardboard or corrugated plastic that the target is affixed to with a stapler or tape). You'll move the target hook up to the firing line and affix the target, then hit the appropriate buttons to move it to the desired distance, all while keeping your gun on the bench and open for inspection. Only after you have positioned your target should you begin loading your weapon and preparing to shoot.

At an indoor range, you never step past the firing line (which would require that you duck under the bench—a big no-no) since the targets come to you. If you are shooting at an outdoor range, the rules are a little different because you have to walk up to the target stands to view your accuracy or to change your targets. Make certain that you or your range officer calls "cease fire," and be sure that everyone's guns are down and empty before you approach the target. On a large outdoor range, it's tempting to go ahead and approach your target if there's someone else shooting far downrange from you, but please resist that temptation. Everyone should have their guns down, no matter where they are standing on the firing line, before anyone approaches a target.

Gun Girl Tip #24

If you shoot primarily on an outdoor range, you might want to invest in a spotting scope, which is basically a telescope that allows you to peer at your target from a long distance in order to assess your hits. They are commonly used in competitive rifle shooting but can be useful with handguns as well. This prevents you from inconveniencing others when you walk back and forth to view your target (thus forcing everyone on the range to cease firing).

Once you actually know which eye to aim with—and you have the proper grip and stance—it is time to acquire your "sight picture" (the proper relationship between the sights and the target). You will do this by focusing on the front sight of the gun. This seems to be the hardest element for many students to understand. You don't look down range at the target, and you don't focus on the back sights. You make sure the front sight is visually sharp and that it is level with the back sights. Those back sights and the target will be blurry. Then you place your front sight over the spot on the target that you want to hit (often the bull's-eye, but not always).

In an NRA basic pistol class, you will learn about breathing, minimizing movement, and a lot of other things that will probably prompt you to overthink the whole process until you have completely lost track of the original (and, in fact, the only) objective: hitting the target. As important as it may be to understand the big picture, here's my best advice: relax. Place that front sight on your target. Don't hold your breath, and don't tense every muscle in your body—just find your sight picture and begin pulling the trigger while maintaining proper grip and stance. Only the pad of your finger should be on the trigger (never the first joint), and you should be surprised when the trigger "breaks" (e.g. when the gun fires). Why surprised? Because if you are anticipating the discharge, you will unconsciously push the barrel down to compensate for the recoil. Most new shooters do it—it's called flinching, and the sooner you recognize and overcome the habit, the better you will be at hitting where you are aiming.

If you plan to shoot more than one bullet, then the goal is to return to your effective shooting form as quickly as possible. If you lose your grip on the gun while firing it, you probably aren't holding it firmly enough, or the gun may be too big or powerful for you. (Don't assume that is the case—usually it is just a matter of getting comfortable with recoil and muzzle flip.) Once the gun has discharged, keep your proper grip, keep your stance, reacquire your sight picture, and *do not* take your finger off the trigger. Yes, I know, your instructors will be harping on you to always keep your finger off the trigger until you are ready to shoot but they do not mean during live fire. If you plan to shoot ten rounds, then your finger stays on the trigger until the tenth round is fired, unless you lower the gun and take your eye off the target. Once the gun fires that first round, you allow the trigger to reset with your finger on it. You will feel the internal click as the trigger resets, at which point you are ready to apply force to the trigger and fire again. This is known as "follow-through," or trigger control. It is one of the most important aspects of accurate shooting. Become comfortable with it, and you will be an accurate shooter before you know it.

As you practice your range shooting, be sure to challenge yourself a bit. Shoot from distances of twenty-one feet or more, but also practice shooting as close as three or four feet from the target. As I have said before, a personal defense encounter will typically not take place from twenty-one feet. It will be up close and personal, and you need to become comfortable pulling the trigger when something is right in your face. You'll be surprised how uncomfortable it can feel shooting at something within arm's reach.

Once you gain skill and confidence, you will want to begin shooting and moving, shooting from behind a barrier, drawing your gun from concealment, and other drills. In the beginning, this is best done at a professional range with a trained instructor. And, of course, check with the staff at your range, and make sure nothing you are doing violates any of their range rules.

But the most important thing you will do on the range is to get comfortable with your gun. Figure out how it works and make certain it functions well in your hands so that you walk away from every range session with the confidence that you can use your firearm effectively.

Another range tip is to always end on a high note. If you are shooting badly at fifteen or twenty feet, pull in the target and focus on accuracy at five feet. The key is to stop when you once again feel competent. Otherwise, it sets up a mental barrier that will plague you when you are not shooting and will impact your skill next time you step up to the firing line. When my husband was preparing to become a training instructor with the Ohio Peace Officer's Training Association (OPOTA), he had a particularly difficult time passing the "El Presidente" course of fire, which was two shots each on three targets, reload, and repeat.

"It was a timed shoot and, if you don't do it successfully in three rounds, you are out as an instructor," John recalled. "I failed the first round and the entire session ended badly. It went downhill from there. When you walk away from the range as a failure, it gets into your head and messes with your confidence. I really focused on my mistake and how, or whether, I could correct it. Naturally, I approached the second round plagued by doubt and uncertainty—so, of course, I botched it too. Then it was crunch time—my career path was hanging in the balance. I knew I could pass the course of fire. I knew I was a good shot. I had just psyched myself into failure. It was becoming a self-fulfilling prophecy."

John wisely sought help for his "shooter's block." But it wasn't one of the guys who ultimately unraveled the knots he had tied in his mind.

"A female OPATA trainer worked with me and showed me how I was psyching myself out and what I needed to do to get back on track. It worked and I passed on my third and final try," John says. "I was relieved, and it taught me a valuable lesson that I use in teaching both law enforcement and civilians—never let the training session end on a sour note. Find a way to pull something positive out so that your mistakes don't climb into your head and live there."

But if too many of your range sessions start to go south, you also need to make sure you are shooting a gun that you *can* be competent with. Sometimes the problem is not your skill but a conflict between your firearm and your body.

I recently had an elderly female student who had already purchased her gun of choice—a Glock 42. On the surface, this should have been a great gun for her: lightweight for carry purposes but not a crazy amount of recoil. It fit well in her hand, and she was even able to rack the slide (after trying a couple different hand positions). The problem was that her wrists were weak and she persisted in limp-wristing the gun, which led to a stovepipe every four or five rounds. The poor lady was so frustrated she was almost in tears, as it became ever clearer that this might not be the best choice for her.

"But the salesman said it was a great gun," she wailed. And the salesman was right, but perhaps not for this particular lady.

Had we simply been test-firing the gun, I would have moved her to something easier, such as the Ruger LCR chambered for .22 Magnum. While I don't think .22s are the best choice for personal defense, it was obvious that this lady knew how to shoot accurately: all of her hits were well within the target area. She simply needed a gun that worked more effectively with the limitations of her aging body.

Since her Glock had already been bought and paid for, I recommended that she spend some extra time on the range working to try to overcome her wrist issues. But not too much time. "Remember that this gun is for your defense. If you don't think you'll be able to keep it from stovepiping, then you need to find something that better meets your needs," I told her.

Your range time is kind of like dating. It should be spent either finding the one that works for you or becoming more comfortable with the one you have chosen. But there sometimes comes a point where you may have to move on to a different model. Just as in dating, the more models you become familiar with—and the more time you spend with the one that strikes your fancy—the sooner you will be able to make an informed decision that won't leave you with regrets down the road. (And, unlike dating, you can always acquire new models as they strike your fancy!)

CHAPTER SUMMARY

- Don't agonize about everything you have to remember. It will become second nature, so long as you practice.

- Take a comprehensive basic pistol class in order to become more comfortable and competent with your gun. But don't stop there; check out reputable ranges, organizations, and gun shops near you for a variety of classes and sessions.

- Know the laws of your state and sign up for legislative updates so that you are always aware of any changes in the law.

- Unless you have asked for help on the range or are doing something unsafe, learn to gently but firmly reject assistance from sometimes well-meaning male shooters.

- Invest in good (and comfortable) ear and eye protection. If you already wear glasses, they are acceptable for range shooting as well.

- Know your dominant eye in order to properly sight in your target.

- Do not "teacup" your grip and always keep both thumbs on the same side of the gun. It may seem awkward at first, but it will prevent hand injuries and will dramatically enhance your control over recoil and muzzle flip.

- Although shooters often use a variety of stances, modern law enforcement prefers the Isosceles stance because of the ability to swiftly and effectively move and shoot from this stance.

- Know the rules of the range where you will be shooting. Follow them to the letter to stay safe and avoid being reprimanded.

- Practice shooting from a variety of distances, especially close up (three to five feet), because that is how close you will likely be in a personal defense encounter.

- Use your range time to become comfortable with your gun—and to make certain it is the right gun for you.

- Always end your range time on a high note, even if it requires doing something very simple and basic.

CHAPTER 9

AFTER THE RANGE

Depending on which gun (or guns) you sampled during your first range experience, you are either feeling ecstatic right now or perhaps a bit let down. Those first shots can set the tone for the rest of your gun experience—if you let them.

If you feel like your hands, wrists, or arms were beat to death, then you may have chosen a gun that is too small or too powerful (or, frequently, both), especially for a first-timer. Don't make the mistake of thinking it will always be that way. Like so many firsts in our lives, ladies, you may not hear angels singing and feel the earth move the first time, but that doesn't mean you won't learn to love it!

But whether your first range time was a total blast or a total bust, you still have work to do. Namely, cleaning the gun, storing it for your next visit to the range, and deciding if—and where—you plan to carry it. If you borrowed a gun, please return it to its owner clean and in full working condition. You might also throw in a box of ammo as a thank-you (as the syndicated columnist, Miss Manners, used to advise: always say thank-you; it makes people want to give more. Cynical—but true.)

CLEANING AND DISASSEMBLING

If this was truly your first time on the range, you are likely thinking "Clean it? I am still figuring out how to fire it!" But, in fact, learning to take apart your gun will only help you understand it better and will hopefully remove some of the mystery.

The good news is that most modern guns come apart and go back together pretty easily. The bad news is, as I noted in our step-by-step tour of your gun, that no two guns break down exactly the same. Each manufacturer seems to believe that it's necessary to add an extra bolt or step in the process, just to keep things interesting.

I love my Springfield XD 9mm because the fieldstripping process is stupid simple (something I can appreciate): First, drop the magazine, then rack the slide back (manually locking it into place by pressing up on the slide lock), inspect the chamber to make sure it is unloaded, then flip down the takedown lever. Next you release the slide and, as you pull the trigger, you simply guide the slide off the front rails. Simple. But, remember to double-check the chamber, because the XD requires you to *pull the trigger* in order to release the slide. The fancier match-grade version—the XD(M)—doesn't require the trigger pull, which makes the process even easier (and safer).

Once you have removed the slide, you can flip it over and pull out the combined recoil spring and guide rod. Under that, you will find the barrel, which also pulls out easily. Lay all the parts on the table, and you are ready to start cleaning. Most guns don't break down any further than this. You *can* remove even more parts—sure, but why would you want to? Modern sprays and cleaners get into the nooks and crannies and keep the internal parts running smoothly. If you truly feel

Once you flip the takedown lever, it becomes pretty easy to break down many modern polymer-framed models.

This is typically as far as you have to "take down" a gun to clean it. This model features a "captured recoil spring" that is attached to the guide rod and is much easier to remove than models with uncaptured springs.

compelled to do so, you can take the gun to a professional every year or so and have them break it completely down for a massive overhaul. I have never done it, and my XD is almost a decade old and still performing like a champ.

Now, unfortunately, not every gun comes apart as flawlessly as the XD. Glocks are similarly simple, as are Smith & Wesson's M&P models. Then you have the other end of the spectrum—the revered 1911, which can appear pretty daunting to the novice. Heck, even my little Walther P22 is a pain in the rear to disassemble because it has an uncaptured recoil spring that rarely wants to feed back into the frame smoothly. More times than I

I love shooting my Walther P22, but I hate taking it apart because I usually have a knockdown, drag out with the uncaptured recoil spring.

can count, the spring has gone flying across the room just as I was about to declare victory. And, instead, I have declared a string of blue words that would make a sailor blush!

When Ruger came out with the SR22 a couple years ago, it offered all the benefits of the P22, with fewer headaches. That included offering a tighter and more easily threaded recoil spring. These days, if I want to shoot .22s (which rarely happens), I usually grab my SR22 over the Walther. It's just not worth the headache of reassembling the Walther.

So—as you consider everything else about the gun that's right for you, be sure you ask the salesman (or woman) about the ease of breakdown. That too can influence how much you ultimately use the gun.

My friend Mike bought a Smith & Wesson Airweight revolver some years back, in part because of the simplicity of loading and carrying it. Once he had fired it a couple times, he began to question his choice. The gun had more recoil than his arthritic thumbs could easily absorb. Moreover, fully loaded with five .38 Special rounds, it was heavier than its "Airweight" name implied—not something he could easily drop into his cargo shorts pocket before setting off on the local bike trail. Not only was it heavier than anticipated but the cylinder of the gun protruded more than he had hoped, creating more potential for "printing" (that is, making the gun's outline visible through clothing). For someone who wanted to carry in a jacket pocket or hip holster, it might have lived up to its intended purpose, but for toting around in cargo shorts while riding a bicycle, it just didn't hit the mark.

But the final straw came when Mike asked a local retired police officer to teach him the proper way to clean it. Mike and I shared an office in those days, and I will never forget the spectacle of our office floor covered by newspaper and two grown men sprawled out with tiny pieces of gun scattered all around them. Mike had simply wanted to know the best steps and products for cleaning the little revolver, post-range time. But our friend Ron wanted to demonstrate a full-scale, top-to-bottom, inside-to-outside cleaning, and he showed up with dental tools and gunsmith's implements. Almost two hours later, the little Smith & Wesson was literally sparkling—inside and out. And Mike was intimidated to the point that he swore he would never shoot the gun again because he had no idea how to replicate Ron's thorough cleaning. The little Airweight languished in Mike's gun cabinet for a few more months before he finally traded it in on a carry gun that suited his needs. And, this time, he didn't ask Ron how to clean it!

The bottom line is that cleaning is a subjective process, and you will be told different things by different people. Our friend Ron was a perfectionist, a former cop who saw the value in keeping his firearms in like-new condition at all times. Mike, too, was a perfectionist, which is why he sought Ron's counsel to begin with. But, the truth is, Ron made it harder than it needed to be—at least for a beginner who simply wanted to know how to keep his firearm in good functioning condition.

A bore snake and a bottle of Hoppe's bore solvent would have done the trick: Run the bore snake through the barrel, back to front, and then run it through each of the chambers in the cylinder. Dip a patch in some Hoppe's and clean the front and back of the cylinder. You may want to use a piece of steel wool on the front, which can get blackened with carbon build-up from the smokeless powder and ensuing explosion.

A bore snake allows you to clean a fixed barrel from back to front.

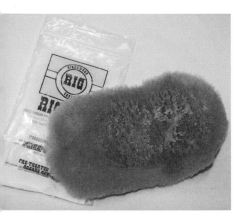

The oil and salt from your fingers can create rust on the metal surface of a firearm. A regular wipe down with a Rig Rag will help protect your gun.

Run a Rig Rag or other cleaning cloth over the whole thing to remove salt residue (from your fingers) and various other impurities, and you have a nice, clean gun—no dental equipment needed. Again, as with the semi-automatic, if you want to send it to a pro every year or two for a micro cleaning, be my guest. Just don't let yourself get so overwhelmed by fear of the breakdown and cleaning process that you simply stop shooting the gun regularly.

Be forewarned—you will get a lot of advice on cleaning. Some good, some not so good. But here is the process taught to me by Ed, my firearms "Yoda." In true Yoda form, he instructed me to "use the force" wisely and gave me much sage advice on shooting straight and shooting safe. I have always followed Ed's guidance on cleaning because I figure that a master instructor (of which there are only a couple dozen in the US) knows as much as anyone and more than most.

But even with Ed, I had to use my own judgment on some advice, such as his assurances that brake cleaner worked great on firearms. I think he may have been flashing back to the all-steel days, because it only took one cleaning with my polymer-framed guns to see that the harsh brake chemicals discolored both the glaze on the slide and the polymer parts of the firearm. Not pretty.

The rest of Ed's advice, however, was spot on, and I continue to follow his routine to this day. As with all the other products named in this book, I am not necessarily endorsing these cleaning products—but I have used them and found them to be acceptable. There are probably equal or better products out there, but this is what works for me. Before you initiate the cleaning process, make absolutely sure there is no ammunition in the area and, most certainly, in the gun!

1. **Disassemble your gun.** You should have received an instruction manual that guides you through this process, but I also encourage you to turn to YouTube, which features hundreds of gun-cleaning

videos. Watch the video a couple times for your specific gun and then walk through the process, starting and stopping the video as needed.

2. **Spray the interior and exterior of the slide with Hornady's One Shot and set aside to marinate.**

3. **Spray the interior of the frame with One Shot and set it upside down so the dirt can drain out.**

4. **Pour some Hoppe's No. 9 or other bore solvent over the bore** brush and run it through the bore. It should be hard to push through. If it glides through easily, the bristles will not effectively scrape residue off the bore. If you are cleaning a gun whose barrel is still attached to the frame, make sure you don't jam the cleaning brush into the breech face (the spot where the firing pin or striker comes out and hits the cartridge's primer cup) or you could damage the firing pin.

5. **Run a Hoppe's-soaked patch through the bore.** You'll thread the patch through the little eyelet attachment that screws onto the tip of your cleaning rod (after unscrewing and removing the cleaning brush). I usually thread the patch dry and then dip the whole thing into Hoppe's once it is secured in the eyelet. Run it through several

One Shot is one of several spray cleaners that help to loosen dirt and debris inside the barrel and action of your gun.

A patch soaked with bore cleaner should be followed by a dry patch until there is little to no visible dirt on the patch.

times—your patch will get blacker and blacker as it scours all the dirt you stirred up with the cleaning brush.

6. **Pull the Hoppe's-soaked patch out of the eyelet and thread in a dry patch.** Run it through several times until it comes out clean (use more than one if necessary).

7. **Use a patch or chamois cloth to wipe down the body of the gun and the interior of the slide, etc.** You may want to use a Hoppe's-soaked Q-tip to get into the nooks and crannies of the slide and the frame, but most of that dirt can be dispelled with a soaking from One Shot (using the little straw attachment that allows you to direct the spray more accurately).

8. **Spray and wipe down the other parts—the recoil spring, bushing (if there is one), and any other detachable parts—and just wipe them off with a chamois.**

9. **Apply oil.** This will go primarily on the outside of the barrel and along the rails of the slide. But you can also run a little oil into the barrel and then run a patch through—you just want enough to protect the interior from rusting. You can oil before you reassemble—or after, which can be easier than trying to assemble a greasy gun. But the thing you *must* know about oiling is how essential is it! I don't know how many times I was told to "add a couple drops of oil" or, worse yet, "add a drop of oil and then wipe it off." Huh? What's the point of that? I tell my students to think about their cars. Has anyone ever advised you to "add a *drop* of oil"? No! You are talking about a machine with moving metal parts that grind against each other and require lubrication to work properly.

10. **Reassemble the gun.**

11. **Wipe down the gun with a chamois cloth and put away (or take out and shoot again!).**

So now your gun is clean. The next question is where are you going to store it? Once again, gun storage is dictated by many factors: where you live, how you live, whether you have children, grandchildren, or a large number of people wandering through your living space.

STORAGE

My husband and I are empty nesters. My son is in college, and I have no grandchildren yet. Since John and I are the only people who have the

Gun Girl Tip #25

I have estimated that 80 to 90 percent of the "broken" guns that come into the shop are not actually broken. Modern guns are very well made, and, while it is possible that the manufacturing process can fail from time to time, it is rare. Yet, weekly we see people with almost-new "broken" guns, and the typical complaint is that ammo is not feeding properly—that is, it is jamming and the slide won't cycle correctly (which is why the ammo won't feed). Well, the first thing we do is rack back the slide and run our fingers along the barrel. And, yep, 80 to 90 percent of the time, it is as dry as the Sahara. The next step is to take the gun into the workroom and give it a quick cleaning (which is usually long overdue) and then lube the heck out of it. Then we head out to our test-fire range to see what's what. I have almost never had the gun replicate the feeding issues. Typically, the now-clean and oiled firearm performs flawlessly. And we have to explain to the owner (who has, by now, mentally acquired the sparkling new model he expects to be handed because we sold him a bum weapon) that the fault lies with the operator and not the equipment.

Every so often oil or dirt is not the only problem—as with the lady who brought in last year's Christmas present, a Kel-Tec P-11, and announced that she had shot it once "and the derned thing is busted"—except she didn't say "derned." She also had spent copious hours on the internet, confirming every bad thing she was thinking about the gun. And, yes, no matter what you think about any given gun or manufacturer, you will find plenty of online ammunition to support your opinion. My advice is to gain your own experience, not trust the rantings of someone you've never met! So, her mild frustration had escalated into an "I've been robbed" mindset. Of course we checked the barrel and, yep, it was bone dry. But she was inconsolable and determined that she never intended to shoot that gun again. After cleaning and oiling it, one of our retired law enforcement salesmen led her back to our test-firing range and watched as she fired it. Oh yeah—her hands were flopping all over the place like a couple of crazed Raggedy Ann dolls. What started as gun repair ended as a training exercise, as our sales guy patiently worked with her on gripping the gun properly, locking her wrists, and controlling the muzzle flip. In a relatively short period of time, she was firing the gun properly and accurately. I don't know if she was thrilled with that discovery, because she had already convinced herself she needed a different gun. But our salesman reassured her that Kel-Tecs are well made (and American made, I might add) utility guns and that she had proven that she could, in fact, shoot safely and well with it. Hopefully, she not only practiced his shooting tips but also took his cleaning and maintenance advice. Yes, there are guns that won't work for you because of their design, power, or cost. But don't blame the gun or the manufacturer for your ineptitude. Proper maintenance and cleaning will make any gun better. Lack of it will destroy even the most expensive firearm.

run of our home, we are fairly liberal with gun placement—when we are at home. We each have a nightstand, and each nightstand has a gun tucked into it when we go to bed. Neither of us is a heavy sleeper or a sleepwalker, both of which can impact where you should keep a gun at night. Something as simple as how fuzzy-headed you are upon awakening might dictate the location of your firearm. Some folks can carry on a conversation for fifteen minutes before they are fully awake. If you are one of those people, having a gun right at your fingertips throughout the night might not be such a great idea. You may be better served to have a small gun safe next to your bed, something that demands a clear head to punch in the combination or finger sequence. That may require a few more seconds of prep time if someone is battering down your door, but, on the flip side, you won't do something stupid in a pre-awakening haze.

We do own a couple of gun safes, but they are full-sized safes for long-term storage and we use them to store our long guns and any pistols that aren't in the personal defense rotation. Both of us typically have a gun within reach at all times in the house. Thankfully, we don't live in a dangerous neighborhood and have never had reason to anticipate problems. Then again, problems can, and usually do, happen when you are least anticipating them.

Now, the moment I have grandchildren, gun placement in our home will change dramatically. That's when I begin shopping for one of a myriad of quick-access pistol safes that will allow me to keep my guns nearby but away from tiny, curious hands.

There are many excellent gun safe models that can be accessed through a variety of quick and easy processes. There are the keypad safes—we have one in our home—where you key in a quick sequence of numbers and turn a knob. This is nice when you are at level yellow and still

Digital safes require you to press your fingers in a specific sequence to access your gun.

This safe is a biometric model, where you slide your finger into the recognition slot and the door pops open. *Photo courtesy of Gun Vault*

unadrenalized enough to remember numbers and use your motor skills. The more stressful the situation, the harder it is to punch those buttons.

There are also the old standard lock-and-key safes. These are pretty easy to open, especially if you leave the key sitting in the lock. The problem with that is, if you have intruders or grandchildren, it is equally easy for them to gain access, as well. If you don't keep the key in the lock, then you stand a good chance of fidgeting wildly while trying to slide it in. Not a good scenario at level orange or above. The keypad and lock-and-key style safes are reasonably priced at roughly $89 on up.

Many of my friends favor the digital gun safes that require you to press buttons in a specific finger sequence. No numbers to remember, no keys to insert, just use your four fingers one after the other—pointer, ring finger, middle finger, pinky . . . or, wait, was it middle finger, pinky, pointer, ring finger . . . or . . . hmm? And so you see the problem: remembering that sequence is no less challenging than remembering your key code, and getting your fingers to apply the necessary force to those buttons can be difficult when your motor skills are abandoning you. I have had trouble in the shop slipping my digits into the finger slots and pressing the buttons when my only real stressor was whether or not I'd make a sale! These safes are made for fingers of average length and strength. Mine don't necessarily measure up—and that could be a problem. Additionally, this safe relies on a battery to keep it functional. If that battery fails you during a break-in, your only option will be throwing the safe at your intruder.

The GunBox RFID and biometric safe allows you to use RFID technology or biometrics, plus it has a battery backup. *Photo courtesy of The GunBox LLC*

Then you have the high-tech variation—a biometric safe. It recognizes your fingerprint and pops open. Very James Bondian! Of course, it also uses battery power and is, therefore, subject to failure at the wrong time. In the early days of these safes, there were complaints that the fingerprint scanning function failed on a regular basis, but those issues seem to have been ironed out, and biometric safes are considered very reliable these days. In good working order, this is your best bet, because all you do is slide your finger in and the safe pops open. It can be programmed for multiple fingerprints so other family members will be protected as well. Pricewise, both this one and the digital safe can be purchased for around $200 and up.

You also have more costly innovations, such as those safes featuring a radio frequency identification (RFID) chip reader or a combination of RFID technology and biometrics. The RFID is an interesting twist but requires you to have the chip in hand. It's the same technology that allows for keyless entry to automobiles. But, again, you lose the chip, and you have lost your access. Having a biometric backup gives you another option in the event that your RFID chip is in the same room with the intruder. These safes start at around $300—but what's the price tag for peace of mind?

The bottom line is that children and guns (without adult supervision) do not mix, and whether you are a parent, grandparent, or auntie, or a BFF whose pal has curious youngsters, it is your obligation as a gun owner to keep those little ones safe.

That having been said, I also oppose the idea of hiding firearms from children. As a mother, I made sure my son knew that we had guns in the house and, at the right age, I made sure he knew why we had them—for hunting, safety, and sport. Obviously, we kept the guns in a locked case out of his reach, but we never pretended that they didn't exist nor did we build them up as something scary or exotic that children must never speak about.

By age eight, Michael was accompanying his father on brief squirrel-hunting jaunts in the woods beside our farmhouse. There, his father would explain the safety elements of proper gun usage to him. I believe Michael was about nine when he was allowed to fire the gun at his first squirrel. I never saw my son misuse a firearm, and I never saw him show an interest in one, beyond using it as a tool. There was no mystery, no need to experiment and test the limits. Michael knew—and knows—that whenever he wanted to shoot, all he had to do was ask, and a parent or stepparent would gladly accommodate him.

So, while you are secreting your guns away in a sturdy safe, make sure your children understand why. Let them know that you keep your gun locked up for the same reason your butcher knife is sheathed in a drawer, your car is locked and garaged, and your medications are on the highest shelf of the medicine chest—so that no one can misuse them or be hurt by them. As long as kids don't view your firearms as something fun you are keeping from them, or, worse yet, as a source of power and control that can resolve interpersonal conflict, then you will be well on your way to raising the next generation of safe and responsible gun owners.

And there you have it. Not only have you cleaned and maintained your gun but you have also stored it in a manner appropriate to your lifestyle and the safety of those around you. Now you can go about your day with the confidence that when you really need it, your gun will be ready to perform.

HOW AND WHERE TO CARRY

At some point you will have to decide whether you want to carry or whether you simply want to have a gun close by when you are at home. If you decide to carry, then you'll need to determine what level of training is required by your state. As you go through the necessary classes and refine your knowledge and shooting skills, you will begin to ponder how you plan to carry your gun of choice.

Women are at a distinct disadvantage when it comes to carrying because we simply aren't shaped like men (thankfully). We are curved

Gun Girl Tip #26

Before he died at eighty-six in 2006, Col. Jeff Cooper was one of the best-known firearms experts in the country. He was a US Marine and the father of the "modern technique" of handgun shooting, in addition to being an international authority on the history and function of small arms. Colonel Cooper developed a color-coded system that identified four levels of situational awareness. Level one is white—which translates into "totally oblivious." Cooper cautioned that you should only be in this condition while sleeping. Unfortunately, too many people spend a healthy portion of their waking hours in the white zone. If attacked while in white mode, your chances of defeat are almost 100 percent. Not a good place to be. The next level is yellow—aware. This is the least alert you should ever be. It means you are comfortable, but paying attention—prepared to take action if the situation warrants it. With firearms within reach and eyes and ears open, my hubby and I are rarely, if ever, out of yellow mode. Even in sleep, we are both likely to be up and alert seconds after an unfamiliar noise filters into our foggy minds. And no, it doesn't feel uncomfortable to live that way. Being in yellow mode means you are aware but still enjoying life. Once you advance to level orange, you have identified a threat and are prepared to dispatch it if necessary. Your nerves are firing and your senses are moving into hyperdrive, but you have not yet taken definitive action. The next step is code red—you are on it. You are taking the necessary action to dispel the threat. You are confident in using deadly force if need be, and there is no hesitation or second-guessing going on. You are committed.

Situational awareness doesn't mean you are a paranoid nutcase; it means you recognize that there are threats in this world and they can arise at any time. As a young woman, I enjoyed going out for drinks with my friends. And, yes, there was more than one occasion when I overindulged, to put it politely. Stinking drunk, if you are telling it like it was. After I became a mother, I cut way back on alcohol consumption because I never wanted to be in a situation where my son needed me and I was unable to respond properly. I knew that my new role as a mother required vigilance and awareness. Although my son is grown now and in college, my personal prohibition against overindulging remains—it is hard enough to respond in a crisis when you are stone-cold sober, let alone when you're two or three sheets to the wind. And, if you have guns in your home, the combination of booze and bullets could be lethal.

Gun Girl Tip #27

The NRA has an excellent training program for very young children. Eddie Eagle helps youngsters understand what they should do if they ever encounter a firearm when a parent is not available, such as in public or at a friend's home. Eddie teaches the children to "STOP! Don't Touch. Leave the Area. Tell an Adult."

The "Stop" and "Don't Touch" commands help your child resist the natural impulse to explore something new. But it is the "leave the area" guidance that I find most useful. How many times have we heard about a child being shot by another child who was inspecting a firearm? Just because *your* child knows the rules of safe gun handling doesn't mean that his or her friends do, and the NRA notes that a child as young as age three has the hand strength to pull the trigger on some guns. It is important that small children get this message of avoidance early and often. "Tell an Adult" makes certain that the incident will not be repeated because a trustworthy adult (preferably a parent but also a neighbor, relative, or teacher) has been informed.

where they are straight; they are firm where we are soft. Unfortunately, you can't bend a gun to fit our curves—it has rigid contours, and a holster has to fit the gun's contours, not ours. In the end, the purpose of a holster is *not* to be a clothing accessory or even to be comfortable—the purpose is to carry and protect a potentially lifesaving tool.

The type of holster or carry device you select will depend on the gun you've chosen and on your lifestyle or mode of dress.

My work puts me in everything from a business suit and pumps to blue jeans and boots. How I carry in a suit is vastly different from how I carry in jeans. Jeans are easy: I tuck my P238 into an inside-the-waistband holster, make sure I have a sweatshirt or jacket over it, and away I go. Or, when I am really looking for quick and easy, like when I take my dog for a walk, I simply drop it into a jacket pocket with a pocket holster snugged over it. You always want to make sure your trigger is covered so you don't inadvertently pull it while fishing around in your pocket. Once again, most concealed carry guns are designed to minimize that potential—but it is still important to do everything possible to eliminate it.

You should also pocket carry only in an empty pocket. Even if you have the muzzle and trigger guard covered, in a crowded pocket you still have the potential that foreign objects could find their way into the holster or, in the case of my P238, could knock the safety off. If you carry a 1911-style gun (as I do), that can be a real problem since these models have a light trigger pull. Carrying "cocked and locked" is essential to safety, so it is imperative that the gun stay locked until you are ready to use it.

If I am out on the range teaching a class, I typically carry in a holster that slides onto my belt. I carry my Springfield XD-9 service

The sturdy Blackhawk holsters with the thumb break are convenient for making certain no one grabs your gun but you. *Photo courtesy of Blackhawk*

model in a Kydex Blackhawk locking holster with a thumb break that prevents others from grabbing my gun, but allows me to depress a button and slide the gun out quickly and smoothly. If you plan to carry in a hard leather or plastic holster with a larger gun such as a full-sized XD, then you will need to invest in a sturdy belt, preferably one specifically designed to support a holster. These belts are typically reinforced to allow for proper weight distribution. Although I have all the right equipment, I still find that my hip aches after I wear the belt and gun for too long. The XD, fully loaded, is no lightweight, and I have a fairly small frame, so I have learned to grin and bear it because I love my XD and am mentally comfortable with it as my range gun.

When my work requires a suit and high heels, my approach to carrying changes dramatically. Many years ago, I purchased a carry purse when they were first becoming popular. At the time, they were mostly big and bulky and just not what I wanted in a purse, but I recently acquired a beautiful handbag made by Gun Tote'n Mamas, a brand we carry in the shop. Today's carry purses come in a range of styles as varied as department store purses—and better made. The model I carry has a steel band sewn into the shoulder strap, which helps distribute weight and also prevents someone from snipping the strap and taking the purse. This particular purse has a front pocket that features a holster attached to the interior panel. In an emergency, I simply slide open the zipper and slip my hand into the pocket. From there, I can pull out my gun or, if needed, shoot through the purse—or, hopefully, simply slide my hand back out once the threat has subsided. No one need ever be aware that my purse is a lethal weapon. Indeed, the exterior pocket that houses my gun is reinforced to eliminate any visible outline. And, once again, I discourage you from carrying anything in the special carry compartment, except for your gun. First of all, you should not be opening that section until and unless you mean to retrieve your gun. Secondly, as with a jacket pocket, items such as tissues, lipstick, keys, or credit cards can lodge in between gun and holster, causing the safety to kick off, the trigger to depress, or lint to creep into the bore of your gun. None of these are good scenarios.

One more little hint that my law enforcement hubby emphasizes to our all-female concealed carry classes: you can (and sometimes should) shoot through a purse or even through a jacket pocket, but please remember that, in all likelihood, the clothing or accessory will catch fire and you will need to ditch it immediately. You must judge for yourself whether you have time to draw from concealment or whether it is imperative to begin firing immediately. But subsequent shots will be harder to make if your hand or hip is rapidly being engulfed in flames!

Choosing to carry in your purse offers both convenience and a level of comfort that usually doesn't accompany on-the-body carry, but it also requires a level of vigilance above and beyond most other forms of carry.

When you have a gun on your waist or in your pocket, it is hard to forget that you have it. It adds extra weight, and it often requires you to slightly modify how you sit or stand. But a gun in the purse is just one more item in an already crowded container.

I used to laugh when I would hear those occasional news stories about some "moron" (my word) who got nabbed with a gun in his briefcase at the airport and used the lame defense "I forgot it was there!"

"How do you forget you are carrying a freaking firearm?" I would mock. Well, I learned how. Several times.

I once carried into my son's high school open house, totally oblivious, until my ex-hubby lifted my purse and gave me a pointed stare, saying in a hushed hiss, "Are you carrying a gun in there?" Oops. Not a proud moment for me, ladies, but I think you deserve honesty, and anyone who has ever carried either has had or will have a moment when the gun becomes such a part of who they are that its presence is too easily forgotten.

The incident that seemed to finally cure me of my forgetfulness came when I was working on a veterans' project that required I visit the local sheriff's office to pick up a proclamation. I rushed over to the facility in between several other errands and hurried into the large multistory building downtown. I smiled at the two armed deputies posted at the entrance and placed my purse on the conveyor belt that fed into a large X-ray machine. Just as the purse was about to disappear between the dangling baffles, I realized in horror that it contained a loaded gun.

Panic-stricken, I dove onto the conveyor and ripped my purse from the bowels of the X-ray machine. Clutching it to my chest, I gave the deputies a wild-eyed stare as I panted, "I have a concealed carry permit! I have to go to my car!" Looking a little perplexed, they both nodded as I loped out of the building toward my car.

At the car, I threw my gun into the trunk, took a couple of deep breaths, and adjusted my suit and hair in an effort to look a little less frazzled. I returned to the building, smiled politely, placed my purse on the conveyor, and passed through the metal detector without a second's hesitation. But it took an hour or so for my heart rate to return to normal.

It makes a good cautionary tale to share with my beginning students— but the truth is, those deputies could have arrested me on the spot. Dressed in a suit and spectator pumps, I probably didn't look like a threat to anyone—but in this day and age, you never can tell. That incident gave me the scare I needed to finally boost my awareness to the necessary level. Today, my work often takes me onto a nearby Air Force base, and I am always acutely aware of my carry status, giving myself ample time to deposit my gun at home before I venture anywhere near the base.

Carrying a gun will become second nature, and whether you carry in a purse or on your person, you have to obey the law and respect the preferences of those who do not welcome firearms.

However, that having been said, I rarely shop at any establishment that does not embrace both me and my firearm. As far as I am concerned, that big red circle and slash with a gun in the middle says loud and clear, "Tara, you and your kind are not welcome here." I am happy to respect their rights, but I also have no intention of financially supporting them. Indeed, I will go out of my way to shop at an establishment that respects my right to carry. When Kroger, the Midwestern grocery chain, made it known that they embraced the rights of concealed carry permit holders, I made sure that the majority of my shopping was done at Kroger. When Panera Bread officials buckled to the anti-gun lobby, specifically the Moms Demand Action group, and announced that guns are not welcome in their establishments, I decided to get my pastries elsewhere.

In reviewing internet commentary on Panera's disapproval of firearms, I noted that a number of folks simply said, "Yeah, I still carry into Panera . . . I just keep my gun concealed." Well, yeah, that's kind of the point! But you are nonetheless violating the right of a private business to serve (or not serve) whomever it chooses and—in my opinion—to trumpet its stupidity (and vulnerability) to the world. I guess I am just stubborn about giving my hard-earned money to anyone who questions or seeks to infringe on my rights as an American citizen. It's that simple. Not to mention that gun owners as a group get a bad reputation when we choose to ignore the law or trample the rights of others who don't favor firearms. But I sure as heck won't help to line their pockets, nor will I place myself or my family in a situation where I could be caught defenseless, as some lunatic (who clearly doesn't care about Panera's policies and preferences) decides to wreak havoc with the weapon of his choice.

I always flash back to the story of Suzanna Hupp and her parents, who were dining at Luby's cafeteria in Killeen, Texas, in 1991 when thirty-five-year-old George Hennard crashed his pickup through the front window and proceeded to systematically execute twenty-three people. Suzanna reached into her purse to retrieve her .38 revolver before remembering that she had stowed it in her glove box in order to comply with the state carry laws! Instead, she watched in horror as Hennard shot her father to death. In the midst of the chaos, Suzanna was able to crawl to safety, believing that her mother was following behind her. Once outside, Suzanna discovered that her mother had chosen to stay with her dying husband, only to be shot in the head at point-blank range by the insane gunman.

And, just for the record, this horrific incident did *not* make Hupp anti-gun—it made her *pro* concealed carry and a passionate advocate for self-defense firearms. She understood the bitter truth that the issue has never been about guns—it is how we deal with criminals; how we instill values, morals, and ethics into our children; how we treat (or ignore) the mentally unstable in our society; and whether we will ever bother to study and understand the true intent of our founding fathers when they framed the Constitution and gave us the right to keep and bear arms.

I always want to obey the law—but I will never forget how Suzanna Hupp's life was forever altered by doing so. So I made up my mind early in my evolution as a pistol-packin' mama to consciously avoid any establishment that does not respect my right to defend myself. Period.

So, you see, just thinking about how you carry and on which body part is not enough. You have to be aware at all times that you are carrying a potentially lethal weapon, and you have to consider where you will and won't go with your precious cargo—and whether you are willing to violate another's right to be stupid (and, believe me, I understand the temptation) or simply invest your hard-earned dollars with like-minded people. For me, it is an easy choice.

If a purse carry option doesn't seem viable, there are many more possibilities to explore.

ANKLE CARRY

I know a lot of cops who carry a small backup gun on their ankles. I've worn an ankle holster just long enough to decide I don't like it. It chafes my leg but, more important, I don't like the idea of having to bend over or kneel down to grab my gun. That movement puts you in an awkward position at a time when you must be at your most nimble and alert. And, for most ladies, unless you have a very lightweight gun, such as a Ruger LCP, Kel-Tec P-3AT, or Taurus 738, trying to walk with an ankle holster may prove downright unpleasant, and it certainly isn't suited to high heels or dress shoes of any kind.

INSIDE THE WAISTBAND

These holsters allow you to carry the bulk of your firearm inside your pants, with only the grip of the gun peeking out (and presumably covered by a shirt, jacket, or vest). Most clothing will accommodate this form of carry, and it is also fairly easy to access. When I carry this way, I usually place the gun in the small of my back, as it seems to fit more comfortably there. I do, however, need to remember not to plop down hard on a seat, as the sudden pressure of steel or polymer against my spine is

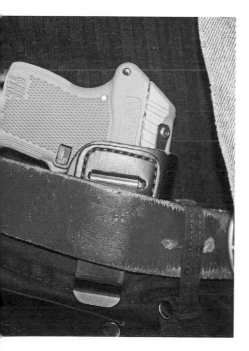

An inside-the-waistband holster is convenient, especially if you have a sweater, sweatshirt, or jacket to cover it.

seriously unpleasant. Note: if you carry in the small of your back, you will need to get a holster designed for the *opposite* of your dominant hand. If I shift my right-handed holster to the small of my back, then suddenly the grip is pointed toward my left hand. But if I place my gun in a left-handed holster and tuck it into the back of my pants, it is easily accessible by my right hand.

Where you decide to place that gun on your body is a personal decision. You have to look at what is comfortable for you. Practice reaching around your back, to your hip, across your abdomen, under your arm or, yes, even into your brassiere to see what works for you.

Before you invest in a holster of any kind, be sure to remove it from the packaging, make certain the texture works for you, and try tucking it where you plan to use it. (Once again, any reputable store will allow this—just be sure you tell the sales staff what you are doing first. You don't want someone to see you stuffing it into your pants and jump to the conclusion that you are stealing it!)

CROSS-CARRY HOLSTERS

These holsters allow you to place the gun on your non-dominant side, with the grip facing your dominant hand. Doing this allows you to reach across your stomach and comfortably place your hand on the grip for a quick draw.

WOMEN'S COMPRESSION CONCEALMENT SHORTS

This is an option that must have been born when someone decided to tuck their concealed carry gun into a girdle and figured out it fit pretty snugly that way! That's essentially what you are getting with these elastic compression undergarments—T-shirts, panties, or, for men, real "tighty whities." The concealed holster is made from surgical-grade elastic and sewn into a pair of real girdle-style compression shorts that keep your gun snugly in place. But be forewarned that the T-shirts and even the underpants can be harder to reach in an emergency. They are hidden beneath your clothing and, in the case of the T-shirt, it will be necessary to reach into or up under your shirt and move your other arm up in order to access the gun. Like the ankle holster, this type of carry does not always lend itself to movement (such as running to escape).

BELLY BANDS

Belly bands offer a versatile and reasonably comfortable means of concealment that is reminiscent of a corset and can be worn low or high. They are made of heavy-duty elastic with a Velcro closure. Most have two firearm slots: one for a semi-auto and one for a revolver. They might

A compression concealment T-shirt hides your gun as well as almost any other type of clothing, but accessing it quickly could be difficult if you have layers on over it. *Photo courtesy of UndertechUndercover*

also contain a pocket that conceals important papers, cash, and credit cards, as well as a built-in mag pouch. The band can be worn around the rib cage (just below the breasts) or literally across the belly and over the hip bones.

What I don't like about these is the difficulty of adjusting or moving the firearm once the band is in place. Likewise, it is located under your clothing and is harder to access than

A bellyband offers a reasonably comfortable means of concealing your gun beneath almost any style of clothing. *Photo courtesy of UndertechUndercover*

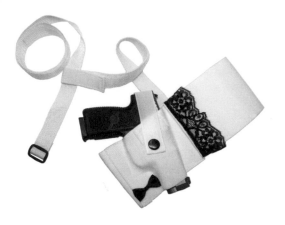

A garter holster may sound sexy, but guns are heavy (even small ones), and I am not sure I'd enjoy this mode of carry. But if you are looking for some sexy security, you'll find it without much looking. *Photo courtesy of Active Pro Gear Inc.*

something that is tucked into your belt, pocket, or purse.

THIGH HOLSTERS

I've never worn one and can't decide whether I ever would. They would have to come with some type of garter belt in order to keep them from sliding down your thigh. Remember, while this has a certain air of "sexy spy lady" to it, even the lightest gun is weighty, and I suspect that keeping it firmly anchored to your thigh would pose a variety of challenges. Still, it is an option to consider if you are a skirt wearer and don't mind the feeling of cold steel between your legs. I'm sorry, it just sounds like a bad detective novel to me! But I have spoken to women who swear by them, so who am I to disagree?

BRA HOLSTERS

These titillating (sorry for the pun) items are designed to be worn either inside the cup or dangling between the girls. They are growing in popularity but I have yet to actively wear one, although I recently purchased a "Flashbang Holster" in case I summon the courage to try. I am especially averse to reaching inside my brassiere to retrieve a lethal weapon, although I have met a surprising number of women who carry all sorts of goodies in their cups. All of them were amply endowed, however, which apparently leaves more room for storage than those of us whose cups range between A and C.

I do see some potential value to the Flashbang model, which attaches to the material between your cups and is secured in place by the lower elastic band of your bra. I am still a bit squeamish about having a loaded weapon dangling so near "the girls," but a Ruger LCP, Kel-Tec P-3AT, or Taurus 738 would all fit nicely there, so long as you are not wearing a formfitting shirt.

The news media recently reported on a woman who was adjusting her bra holster and managed to kill herself with a shot to the eye. While I don't know the details of this incident, I can tell you that adjusting a loaded weapon on your body (wherever you may be carrying it) requires focus and caution. It's not like blindly hiking up your panty hose or twisting your slip back into place. You don't fumble with a gun beneath your clothing, and you *never* point the barrel toward yourself or anything you don't plan to shoot. Somehow, she managed to turn the barrel toward her face as she was looking down. It was a fatal mistake but it was certainly not the manufacturer's fault. Carrying a loaded firearm requires added vigilance. If you aren't willing and able to apply the necessary caution, then—for your sake and the sake of those around you—please do not carry.

Moving south from the chest region, there is some value in the holster style that replicates a cell phone case or fanny pack. My sister is a big fan of the fanny pack because it is a convenient purse substitute when she is out for a run. Once again, your firearm of choice would need to be as small and light as possible—especially if you are a runner. I'm not sure I would want a gun flopping up and down across my fanny or tummy. On the flip side, however, a fanny pack is highly accessible (to you, but not to others) and is not as likely to be snatched off your person as a purse might be.

For business professionals, holsters hidden in briefcases and day planners are carry options that might be useful, but they have their own set of limitations. Unlike a purse, these items have no strap and no way to attach to the body. More problematic, a briefcase or day planner usually gets tucked away and forgotten for much of the day. You definitely shouldn't walk away from it if it is hiding a firearm. On the plus side, if a bad guy is going to snatch something, it will almost always be your purse, since that is typically where he will find your cash, credit card, keys, etc. There aren't a lot of carry briefcases and day planners available, but some manufacturers do make them. Once again, your lifestyle should dictate the carry location that would be best for you.

DRAWING FROM CONCEALMENT

Once you have settled on your preferred location and method of carry, you will need to make a point of practicing drawing from concealment, wherever that may be. And you don't have to be on the range to do this. So long as you remember to unload your firearm, you can easily perfect your technique from the comfort of your own home. Make sure you practice with various types of clothing on, so you can assess where the challenges lie.

As you are testing your skill drawing from concealment, this is also a good time to brush up on your stance, grip, and trigger pull through dry-firing exercises. Dry firing means practicing all the elements of

If you practice dry-firing with a coin atop the barrel of your gun, it will help you to master a smooth trigger pull.

shooting—without ammo.

Once again, before you start yanking the trigger, make sure the gun has been thoroughly cleared (checked for ammo) and that no ammunition is anywhere nearby.

With a revolver, dry firing is a simple process. Place a dime or a quarter atop the flat front sight of the gun (this won't work if it has a blade, but you can also place the coin atop the barrel near the front sight if there is a flat surface), bring the revolver up, making sure you have the proper grip, and focus on that front sight and the sight picture before you begin pulling the trigger repeatedly, working to be so smooth with your pull that you don't knock the coin off its perch.

Practicing this ten or fifteen times per night will have a significant impact on the smoothness and consistency of your trigger pull and, therefore, your accuracy.

You can practice the same technique on semi-automatic pistols but the process is a little different (mainly because you have to remove the coin each time you rack the slide—or you can ditch the coin and simply practice your trigger pulls). Unlike a live-fire exercise, the slide won't be moving, at least not by itself, but you can still use these sessions to become familiar with your trigger's reset sound and sensation.

When you are firing repeatedly, you do *not* keep taking your finger off the trigger. In fact, you shouldn't even let the trigger return to its resting position. Instead, you allow it to move forward only until you hear/feel the reset and have reacquired your sight picture; then you are ready to fire again. So what does that look like in a dry-fire scenario?

1. Rack the slide and acquire your grip and sight picture.

2. Pull back the trigger until it "breaks" (the click that would initiate the firing sequence if the gun were loaded).

3. Leave the trigger depressed, as you reach up and rerack the slide (you don't have to pull it all the way back; just a short yank should recock it).

4. Reacquire your sight picture and allow your trigger finger to move forward until you hear/feel the reset.

5. Immediately pull the trigger back to refire.

It sounds like a lot of work, but it actually helps. You can also use this exercise to practice keeping both eyes open while sighting. Simply acquire your sight picture with your dominant eye, then slowly open your non-dominant eye as you keep the front sight framed within the back sights.

Even if you can't get to the range regularly, these exercises will keep you comfortable and familiar with your firearm.

The final concealed carry exercise doesn't involve your gun at all, but it is essential to successful carrying. Before you go out in public with a loaded firearm, make certain you know the laws of your state. I would even go so far as talking to your local police department about any special practices they prefer from their concealed handgun license owners.

In a traffic stop, law enforcement will know you are a CHL holder before they ever approach your car (it will come up when they call in your plates). The onus is on you to make sure it is one of the first pieces of information you volunteer.

The proper exchange would be, "Good morning, officer. I am a concealed carry permit holder and I am carrying a gun in my purse. What do you want me to do?" The *improper* technique would be rolling down the window and shouting to the approaching officer, "I have a gun!"

I also advocate wrapping your thumbs around the top of the steering wheel and keeping your fingers extended upward as the officer approaches your car—that way he knows where your hands are at all times.

Do not fumble around for your license while he is approaching the car. Remember, he has every reason to believe you have a weapon in your possession.

If your gun and your driver's license and registration are in the same place, you will have to wait for instructions from the officer. Usually it is not an issue. He will likely tell you to leave the gun holstered and reach into your purse for the driver's license. Do so slowly and carefully.

If you happen to get stopped by a nervous or control-freak officer, you may be asked to surrender your firearm for a period of time. It is not worth the hassle to argue. Bring the firearm out slowly and hand it to the officer (grip first please—*never* point the muzzle in his direction). Don't argue or give him a dissertation on your rights. If you feel his behavior is really out of hand, pay a visit to his precinct or office and lodge a complaint with his superior. Despite what you see in the media, good cops don't tolerate or cover for bad cops. If his behavior indicates a pattern of abuse, his superiors will need—and want—to know.

But you are not the only person who needs to be aware of your concealed carry status when driving: any family members who will use your car also need to be briefed. If you are Suzy Smith and your daughter, Sarah Smith, frequently drives your car, a law enforcement officer won't know she isn't you until he reads her driver's license. Therefore, again, he will have every reason to believe that she is armed. She will need to follow the same procedures I have outlined for you, except that she will say, "Officer, this is my mother's car. She has a concealed carry license but I do not, and there are no guns in this car."

Don't assume that your son or husband is immune, either. Everyone who drives your car needs to know the drill and observe it.

In the end, concealed carrying is not something you do sometimes—it is a lifestyle and it requires adjustments on the part of you *and* your family. But in a scary and unpredictable world, it levels the playing field—for women especially, but for anyone who believes in the right of citizens to defend themselves.

Be smart. Prepare yourself. Invest in good equipment and good training. Ask questions. Practice. Practice. Practice. And you, too, will find the peace and protection that comes from being a gun girl.

CHAPTER SUMMARY

- Learn to be at ease with the process of dismantling and reassembling your firearm; use your manual and instructional videos on YouTube to become more familiar with the process.

- Clean your firearm regularly and remember to apply oil.

- Figure out a home storage method for your gun based on your lifestyle, neighborhood, and the number (and age) of people who have access to your home.

- Train yourself to live in a "code yellow" situationally aware state.

- If you have young children, make sure they are aware of safe gun handling practices through one-on-one instruction from you as well as through exposure to the NRA's Eddie Eagle.

- Decide what kind of holster and what location on the body works best for you.

- Remember that frequent carrying will lead to a comfort level with your firearm. While it is good to be comfortable, you must always be alert to situations or locations where you are not permitted to carry.

- Obey the law and respect the rights of others who do not approve of firearms, but avoid placing yourself in a situation where you are vulnerable. I simply don't shop at stores that have declared their opposition to our carry laws. I won't violate their rights but neither will I surrender mine.

- Dry-fire practice in your home will help with trigger control, sight picture, and follow-through.

- Practice drawing from concealment under a variety of clothing styles.

- Make sure any family members who drive your car are aware that you have a concealed carry permit. Brief them on how they should behave and what they should say if pulled over by a police officer.

CHAPTER 10

HOW TO VISIT A GUN SHOP

I am ever amazed by the hesitance of many women to walk into a gun store. I have been greeted by gasps of relief and even a hug or two from female customers who are relieved to find a little estrogen behind the gun counter.

The men that I work with are competent, caring individuals who truly want to help customers of all genders find their perfect gun. But they are guys, and they simply don't fully comprehend the discomfort that women may feel when treading on masculine hallowed ground.

When I told my husband I was adding a section of the book titled "How to Visit a Gun Shop," he gave me a strange look. "What'll it say—drive to the shop, get out of your car, walk into the shop?" he teased. But he, too, as a gun store manager, has dealt with the hesitation and uncertainty of new female shooters. More important, he has been with me when we have visited other gun shops. He watched in Florida as I did everything but climb on the counter and scream, in an effort to get one of a multitude of male sales people to wait on me—yet when he approached the sales counter, he was waited on in a matter of seconds. So he knows. Despite the good-natured teasing, he knows.

So I suppose this advice would be better labeled "What to Look for in a Gun Store" or "What to Expect from a Firearms Salesperson."

First of all, take note of whether you are greeted by someone when you enter the store. They don't have to fawn all over you and roll out the red carpet, but they should at least acknowledge your presence, especially if they are not busy waiting on other customers.

Once you have begun to browse, someone should ask if you need assistance. Firearms are rarely out where you can handle them, so it is incumbent on the sales staff to hand you anything you might like to see.

I would recommend that you do your gun shopping in a store where the sales staff works on salary, rather than commission (and don't be afraid to ask). That way, you can be fairly certain that the gun your salesman is recommending truly fits your stated needs and not his quota for the month.

Don't hesitate to ask for a salesperson who is especially attuned to assisting new shooters. We all have our areas of expertise. If someone comes in with reloading questions, I point him toward Randy; skeet or trapshooters go to Scott; revolvers and 1911s fall into Bob's lap; and so on.

There is likely someone in the shop that you are visiting who has more experience guiding new shooters. That individual may be male or female, but the important thing is that he or she has empathy for your lack of knowledge and is experienced at drawing out novices with the right questions and observations.

I compare the gun-buying experience to shopping for computers. I once almost got into a fistfight with a computer salesman (not my finest moment) who was stubbornly trying to steer my friend Mike toward a computer that was the exact opposite of the need Mike had described. It was three times the price we had requested and had bells and whistles that we had already established were not needed. But Mike's knowledge of computers was comparable to that of any novice shooter's grasp

Don't judge a shop by what it looks like on the exterior—judge it by the service you get once inside. *Tami Freed/Shutterstock*

of firearms. Despite my objections and repeated explanations to the salesperson, he persisted in trying out his razzle-dazzle two-step on Mike. We exited the store rather quickly, after Mike was forced to step between me and the determined salesman.

Once I had calmed down, we headed to a competing computer store where a young salesman listened intently to Mike's description of his computing needs and directed him to a model that was exactly what he needed. I was so overjoyed that I hugged the young man and thanked him for his responsiveness. I have always suspected that salesman number one was commissioned (with a bad attitude, to boot) and salesman number two was salaried. If salesman two *was* on commission, then he was richly rewarded for his performance, since we left the store carrying a new computer, a printer, several expensive pieces of software, and a variety of other computer accessories.

I am always reminded of an observation made by aviation legend and savior of Learjet Harry B. Combs, who once told me, "We live to serve . . . and those who serve the best, live the best." And thus it is with any sales, but especially with gun sales where, today, there are so many retailers to choose from.

You are the customer and you have every right to expect good service and good advice. Don't get me wrong—the salesman doesn't have to be touchy feely. We have warm, fuzzy guys at the shop and we have gruff, competent guys, and, of course, everyone has a bad day from time to time. I always try to give any shop or salesman a second chance (with the exception of my wildly aggressive computer salesman).

Don't be afraid to ask questions—a lot of questions if need be. And, in the end, if your salesperson is dismissive, disinterested, or disrespectful, please tell him (or her) that you have decided you should spend your money elsewhere. And, if you feel so inclined, tell his manager or the shop owner as well. That gives them the opportunity to make things right, not necessarily by giving you something but by meeting your original needs.

If all goes well and you decide to make a purchase, make sure you ask the salesperson to walk you through the process of taking your gun apart. You probably won't remember everything once you get home, but at least you have a foundation of knowledge to build on.

Before you actually pay for your firearm, you will be presented with a government document that must be filled out and signed. In most states, this does not "register" your gun. This merely gives permission to have your background checked. You will answer such classic questions as "Are you a fugitive from justice?" or "Have you been declared mentally incompetent?" The *real* question is, if you were either of those things, would you be stupid enough to tell me?

Don't be intimidated by the form. It is six pages long, but, as with most government forms, 80 percent of the document is an explanation of how to fill out the other 20 percent. You will fill out the front page and will sign at the top of page two. Everything else will be completed by your salesperson. No need to worry that your traffic tickets or late fees will impede your gun ownership. If you are felony-free and have never been cited for domestic violence, you should sail through the process. It takes about ten minutes to be approved, after which, you are free to purchase your firearm, except in states that have a waiting period. But, be forewarned: every single day we have law-abiding citizens who walk into the shop, fill out the paperwork, and are given the news that their approval process has been delayed!

It is disconcerting and a little embarrassing, but it is rarely anything but a formality. Usually, the delay results from someone else somewhere else who has your same name but has not lived your exemplary life. Including your social security number on the form can help but is also not a guarantee of approval.

If you are delayed, that delay is typically lifted within four days and you are free to come back and pick up your gun. Usually, if you are delayed one time you will be delayed every time you purchase a gun. To prevent such routine delays, you can apply for a Unique Personal ID Number (UPIN) through the FBI. There is a spot on the form for you to fill in your UPIN, which usually resolves any identity confusion.

Just please remember that the sales staff has no control over who is or isn't delayed. We simply do what the Feds tell us to do—and, yes, if we fail to do so we are out of business. Even if we know you to be a pillar of the community, it won't change the delay until and unless the Feds approve you.

One other reminder: if the address you have written on the form is different from the address on your driver's license, be prepared to produce a second government-issued document that features your new address. That can be a change of address card from the Bureau of Motor Vehicles, a car registration, or a hunting or fishing license, but not an electric bill or insurance card. In Ohio, we can sell you a pass to a state-run range for $5, and that serves as your second government document. But it might be easier to just go get your driver's license changed to your new address before you head to the gun shop.

If you are uncomfortable walking into a gun shop cold, then call ahead and see about making an appointment with someone specifically

I loved my time behind the gun counter at Olde English Outfitters. It offers some of the best customer service I've encountered at a gun store, but thankfully, there are others out there with an emphasis on the customer.

trained to assist new shooters. Olde English offers this kind of personal shopping service, and it is truly the wave of the future in a world where micromarketing and customer service will make or break retailers.

There are advantages and disadvantages to both big-box stores and mom-and-pop outlets. In a big-box store, you are likely to get a salesperson who was selling shoes or camping gear two days earlier and knows little about firearms, while the mom-and-pop shops, unless they have been around a long time, may not have the buying power and relationships with distributors to get you the best prices and the broadest selection of models.

One final caution: many, if not most, of today's firearms retailers offer some type of classes, whether they be concealed carry, introductory classes, or advanced shooting. Just because a shop sells guns does not make it qualified to sell training. Make sure the instructors are NRA certified, preferably retired law enforcement or military, and skilled presenters as well. Not everyone who understands firearms is suited for teaching.

There may be a period of trial and error as you attempt to find the best possible fit between yourself and a competent, customer-oriented retailer. But once you have found that fit, you will be rewarded with expertise and insight that will take you from your awkward beginner questions through your evolution as a safe, savvy, and seasoned gun girl.

CHAPTER SUMMARY

- Don't settle for shopping in a gun store where you are ignored or, worse yet, treated like a half-wit!

- You don't need touchy-feely salespeople, but you should expect—and demand—competent, thorough ones.

- Your paperwork might come back as "delayed" but don't panic; it happens to a lot of very nice folks who are almost always approved after a couple days.

- If you are repeatedly delayed, you can secure a "UPIN" (unique personal identification number) through the FBI.

CHAPTER 11

WOMEN AND GUNS— A LAW ENFORCEMENT PERSPECTIVE

Women can sometimes be their own worst enemies when it comes to firearms and personal defense. We either count on others to defend us or we simply choose to believe that nothing bad can happen. Both scenarios have the potential to be both disappointing and dangerous.

Multiple times, I have had female customers (who were usually in the shop at their husband's or boyfriend's behest) look me in the eye and say, "I don't need to learn to defend myself—that's what the police are for."

Uh, no.

If the police existed to defend us, we would all be issued our own personal cop at birth.

Few of my law enforcement buddies would argue with the oft-quoted chestnut, "When seconds count, the police are minutes away." And it's true, because law enforcement does not exist to prevent crimes but, rather, to clean up the messes created by crime and to capture the criminals. Now, they certainly work to minimize criminal incidents through education, patrols, and penalties—but they are by no means here to make sure you are safe, especially when you do stupid things.

I can't count the number of times I have watched perfectly intelligent, successful women decide that they are safe going for a run at night without any defensive item on their person. And too often, the place they choose to run is questionable even during the day. This is particularly true among the college set, where women tend to feel more protected and thus free to drink heavily and stumble back to the dorm alone. A recent high-profile murder case showed the folly of that particular choice. Now I am not recommending that you go drinking *and* carry a loaded gun. Not only is it illegal, but it's just plain dumb. I am, however, suggesting that women need to think more clearly about the choices they make with regard to personal safety. One of those choices should be to at least consider learning to shoot. A gun in trained hands is no more dangerous (and probably less so) than an automobile or any other tool that can be misused.

Our world is not safe. In fact, it never has been. There have always been nefarious sorts who want to do harm as a means to an end—or just for fun. Whether or not you wish it weren't so is immaterial. It is what it is. You can pretend that we are one big, happy world where the denizens of the forest cavort and sing with us as we dance our way through life. Or you can acknowledge that bad people do bad things and that you would like to prevent them from doing such things to you or your loved ones.

Once you make that emotional leap into being responsible for your own safety, life gets a lot simpler. As a person of faith, I put a great deal of trust in God. But I also believe that God put everything on earth that I might need in order to live a safe and productive life. That includes guns. Inanimate objects have no conscience or intent; whether they are used for good or evil depends entirely on the hands holding them.

Being married to someone who spent twenty-eight years in law enforcement—and having had the chance to get to know other LEOs through my gun work—I can tell you that the majority of police are fine with the concept of concealed carry. In most states, having that license means you have had at least some training and, more important, that you respect the rule of law enough to go through the process.

Indeed, my husband and many other LEOs wish that more women would take responsibility for their own safety.

"I can't count the number of times in my career that I was called in to clean up a situation that could have been avoided if the victim was armed and trained," John tells me. "It is frustrating and disheartening when you know the scenario could have been—*should* have been—different."

But he has seen it again and again.

"Too many women don't pay attention to their surroundings. Go to the mall or supermarket and look around you. They are texting, chatting on the phone, rooting around in their purses, or window shopping, completely unaware of what—and who—is going on around them. Men are guilty of the same thing, but men don't become victims with the same regularity that women do," John explains. "Predators look for prey who are compromised and unaware. Watch any show on the National Geographic channel and you will see evidence of it in nature. Well, like it or not, we have that in common with the animals. Our predators seek to identify and isolate the weak or distracted—and then they attack."

But women with guns present a more confident and aware attitude, John says. "It is partly because of their training and partly because they wouldn't be carrying if they didn't understand the need for vigilance."

Gun laws are different from state to state, but John tells our students that common sense transcends state boundaries.

"If you find yourself in a personal defense encounter, it will happen so fast that it will be very difficult to process. Police officers go through this every day, and you cannot understand the need for split-second decision making until you are placed in that situation," he says. "Your mind will be racing, along with your heart and your breathing. Your entire body will be reacting to the twin forces of adrenaline and fear. This is why you need to practice with your gun, because when you really need it, all you will have is instinct. If using that gun isn't instinctive, you will have a big problem."

John tells our students that their first responsibility is *not* to draw and shoot—it is to get away. "I don't care if your state requires a 'duty to retreat' or tells you that you can 'stand your ground,' you still want to avoid a confrontation, if at all possible. Believe me, you don't want the emotional angst that comes with shooting and killing another human being, no matter how well deserved it might be," John explains. "And you cannot predict how any situation will unfold. The only thing you can be sure of is that escaping the confrontation will eliminate a variety of unpleasant scenarios. Your goal is to make certain that, whatever happens, you are still standing when it's over."

I recently read an article in a popular gun magazine by a lawyer who was offering advice to concealed carry permit holders. Among his gems of wisdom was that, in the event of a confrontation, you should keep your gun at the ready, even after you have dispatched the bad guy, "because you never know if he has an accomplice nearby. Always be ready for another gunfight." This fellow also pointed out that "leaving the scene is always viewed as an admission of guilt."

I read these tips to my husband, who shook his head vigorously. "Spoken like someone who has never been in a gunfight," he said.

John's advice to my students always leaves a few of them startled and asking questions. It is not what you would expect—and it does not apply to every situation. But it does have a ring of common sense and the wisdom of someone who spent many years dealing with the aftermath of shootings.

"If you are ever in a situation where you are out in public and have to shoot someone in self-defense, leave the scene immediately," John says. What? Isn't that why they charge people? But he continues. "Leave the scene and call 911. If there is a restaurant or café nearby, go and order something to eat. Tell the dispatcher that the police can find you there to take a statement. The most important thing you can do is to stop the events from looping in your head and distorting your thought process. You won't be fit for anything until you regain control of your mind and body. Eating is a familiar activity that will reorient your senses and calm those inflamed nerve endings," John explains.

"Plus, the police do not know the situation when they arrive on scene—it is chaotic and all they will see is that you are standing over a dead or disabled body. They have no idea in those initial moments whether you are the aggressor or the defender. That concern is ridiculously magnified if you are still holding a gun. It's crazy to advise someone to remain on scene and be 'ready for another gunfight.'"

And yes, there is a chance that your attacker may have an accomplice, which is all the more reason to get the heck outta Dodge. You are a civilian and are neither experienced nor conditioned to endure multiple gunfights. You will be a mess if you have to use your gun once, let alone sticking around to have another go at it.

And when the police do arrive to take your statement, that statement should be brief. You will be adrenalized and upset. "He threatened me with a knife to my throat and tried to drag me into the alley. I shot him until he stopped," is sufficient, followed by "I want to talk to a lawyer." Or, simply, "I was in fear for my life. I shot him until he stopped. I want to talk to a lawyer."

The bottom line is that every situation is different. You may be arrested until the police can sort things out. In some cases you may even be charged. Carrying insurance specifically designed for concealed carry holders is not a bad idea, as you may be forced to defend your actions in a court of law.

John's "leave the scene" advice does not apply to a shooting that occurs in your home. Over thirty states recognize a self-defense theory known as the Castle Doctrine. This legal doctrine provides that a person's residence (or, in some states, vehicle, hotel/motel room, or even workplace) is a location where he or she is protected from prosecution in the event that he/she uses force (including deadly force) to defend against an intruder. Typically, deadly force is considered justified if the individual can reasonably assert that he or she feared for his or her life or serious bodily harm. That last part is important because it includes such life-altering events as rape.

The Castle Doctrine is not a law, per se, but a set of principles used to assess a situation.

"Leaving your own house after a shooting is not a good idea," John explains, "because you don't know what's waiting for you outside. In this case, set down the gun, make the call to 911, don't touch the crime scene, and go grab a handful of chips or something that will distract you from the intensity of the moment."

John advises concealed carry permit holders to be prepared for a variety of scenarios if they are forced to use their gun in self-defense, including civil suits from family members of the deceased intruder.

"Plenty of people will want to second-guess your actions, or try to take advantage of them for personal gain," he advises. "But the bottom line is and always should be—you are the one left standing—you are the one who is there to tell the story. Everything else can be overcome. Death is permanent."

CHAPTER SUMMARY

- Ladies, we are responsible for our safety. Don't do stupid things repeatedly and expect to be saved. Sooner or later, the law of averages will bite you on the rear.

- Learn to be situationally aware. Pay attention to what is going on around you at all times.

- Your first obligation in a personal defense encounter is to avoid an armed confrontation in any way possible. Even if your state allows you to "stand your ground," if you can escape the conflict without having to draw your firearm, do so.

- If you are forced to defend yourself, your next obligation is to be the one who lives to tell the story.

CONCLUSION

I started this book mainly to fill a void that I found when I was learning to shoot—namely, the lack of printed material geared toward new shooters and, specifically, new female shooters. I bought book after book that explained some aspects of shooting but always seemed to assume a certain level of knowledge on other elements. I wanted to be guided, step by step, through the various decisions I needed to make regarding firearms and whether or not to carry. I didn't want someone to tell me what I should do, but I very much wanted to understand what my options were. I just wasn't finding those answers in many of the male-oriented firearms books. Likewise, I wanted to hear from someone who had asked (or, more importantly, hadn't asked) all the stupid questions and could understand why women sometimes hesitate to speak up. I wanted to get as close to a step-by-step guide as I could, while still generating an interesting read.

As I wrote, the book became something more. It became an homage to the people who had taught me to shoot—to my ex-husband and his family who taught me that guns were not something to be feared; to my employer, Evan English, who took a chance on me when I was trying to expand my knowledge and experience with firearms; to my husband (who, incidentally, became my husband in no small part because of my interest in guns) and his never-ending patience and instruction; and to all the ladies (and the gents) whom I have instructed through the years; they've taught me that I still have plenty to learn and that there are no stupid questions—except those left unasked.

The book has also become, I hope, a clarion call to women that it is time we took responsibility for our own protection and that of our families. When we surrender our personal safety to authority figures or to pure dumb luck—we are saying, in essence, "I don't deserve a level of protection that is proactive and forceful," and we place our protectors in a terrible position if they are not available when we need them most. The right to self-defense should be an essential part of equal rights. My guns are tools in my everyday life, and they have no conscience or will, save what I impose on them.

ASK AN EXPERT

A coworker recently introduced me as a "gun expert," which prompted me to laugh out loud. I am by no means an expert. Indeed, true experts are few and far between. Colonel Jeff Cooper was an expert; the rest of us have our "areas of expertise." Mine seems to be translating the complexities of handgun usage to beginners. I certainly have specific models and gun-related topics with which I am very familiar, but that doesn't make me an expert. And even the experts have their weaknesses; that's why it pays to listen to a variety of people and to take classes taught by a variety of instructors.

What I am good at, however, is knowing who to ask. And I am blessed to know a number of folks who have spent far more time in the trenches of gun handling than I. So if you have waded through this entire book and you still have questions, I want to be able to respond to them, either by sharing my own experience or by seeking the counsel of someone who has first-hand knowledge.

To aid your efforts in no-nonsense language, I have created a web site and Facebook page: www.gungirls.org and www.facebook.com/gungirlsbook. Feel free to peruse both and to send me your questions, comments, and concerns.

I had a lot of "stupid questions" (they weren't really) when I was just starting out, and I could find no place where I could anonymously ask for an explanation. I also quickly discovered that there are many subjective responses to gun-related questions. I will try my darndest to give you the closest thing I can muster to a definitive answer, but I can assure you that my own experiences and gun prejudices will no doubt play a part, as well.

As I have said multiple times in this book, don't be afraid to venture into your local gun shop and ask questions. If the guys behind the counter (and most of them will be guys) are not cooperative, well, then you have learned where you don't want to spend your hard earned money. I am sure the friendly folks at Olde English Outfitters would be happy to talk to you.

GLOSSARY

ACP: An abbreviation meaning Automatic Colt Pistol. It is commonly used to designate specific calibers, particularly those originally designed by John Browning, such as .45 ACP, .380 ACP, and .25 ACP.

action: The moving parts of a firearm that cartridge for firing, and removing the spent casing and introducing a fresh cartridge.

ambidextrous mag release: A button or lever for dropping the magazine out of the gun that is located on either side of the firearm (or, in the case of a Walther, directly on the trigger guard as a lever that can be pressed by one or more fingers).

ambidextrous safety: An external manual safety that can be activated using either hand, usually via a tab or lever located on either side of the upper back of the firearm.

ammo: Short for ammunition.

ammunition: The entire element that is composed of a primer (which acts as a fuse), a charge of propellant (gunpowder), and a projectile (bullets, slug, or pellets), all wrapped in a case or shell. A single unit of ammunition in modern firearms is called a cartridge. The unit of measure for quantity of ammunition is a round. The ammunition used must match the caliber of the firearm, and you can make certain by checking the head stamp (flat, circular bottom of the ammo).

automatic weapon: A gun designed to feed cartridges, fire, eject the empty cases, and repeat this cycle until the trigger is released. In an automatic, one trigger pull could fire thirty rounds, whereas with a semi-automatic, you would have to pull the trigger thirty times in order to discharge thirty rounds. Some folks refer to semi-automatic pistols as "automatics," but they are not true automatics.

backstop: Dirt, tires, hay bales, rubberized coatings, or anything that safely prevents a bullet from continuing on its path once the target is hit.

back strap: The rear surface of the grip, which fits into the palm of your hand.

ballistics: The science of cartridges and bullet flight. Internal ballistics focuses on what happens inside a firearm upon discharge, external ballistics studies a bullet's flight, and terminal ballistics is the study of the impact of a bullet.

barrel: The metal tube through which the bullet travels. The barrel provides direction and builds velocity for the bullet.

battery: A firearm is said to be in battery when the breech is fully closed and locked, ready to fire. When the breech is open or unlocked, the gun is out of battery. A semi-automatic is out of battery when the slide fails to come all the way forward again after the gun has fired, making it dangerous or impossible to fire the next round. This condition can be created by a misfeed, a dirty gun, riding the slide, or various other causes.

beavertail: A large piece of curved metal at the top of the grip that protects the user's hand from slide bite.

black powder: The earliest propellant, which has mostly been replaced by smokeless powder, except in some muzzleloaders and older breechloading guns.

bluing: The chemical process of artificial oxidation (rusting) applied to gun parts so that the metal attains a dark blue or almost black appearance.

bore: The interior part of the barrel through which the bullet travels during its acceleration phase.

bore diameter: The diameter of the inside of the barrel after boring, but before rifling.

brass: A slang term for an empty shell casing. Most shell casings are made of the metal alloy known as brass.

breech: That portion of the gun that contains the rear chamber portion of the barrel. The rearmost end of a barrel, closest to the shooter.

breech face: Internal surface of the gun out of which the firing pin protrudes in both revolvers and semi-automatics.

breech-loading firearm: A firearm in which the cartridge loads into a chamber at the rear of the barrel.

bull barrels: Barrels that are not tapered and are very thick. Target pistols, such as the Browning Buck Mark or the Ruger Mark III, often have bull barrels to aid in accuracy.

bullet: The metal projectile fired from a gun. It is not the same as a cartridge; the cartridge is a complete package—consisting of the case, primer, powder, and bullet—which is typically referred to as a round. Bullets can be various shapes, weights, and constructions, such as solid lead, ball-tip, hollow-point, wadcutter, etc.

butt: The base of the grip on a handgun.

butt plate: The base of the magazine, which can typically be slid off (carefully, because of the taut spring) so that a different style butt plate (flat or with a pinky extension) might be added.

cable lock: A cable with a padlock at the end. It is threaded through the action of the firearm.

caliber: The diameter of the bore of a firearm measured as a fraction of an inch, although in Europe and sometimes in the United States, such a measurement may be stated in millimeters. It is expressed as ".40 caliber" (note the decimal point) or as "10 millimeter" (without "caliber" or the decimal point). Caliber numbers are often followed by a description of the round (Magnum or Special) or a manufacturer's name (Smith & Wesson or Sig), or, in some cases, another number or even the name of an individual.

cartridge: A single, complete round of ammunition, which includes the case, primer, powder, and bullet.

case: The container portion of a cartridge that wraps around all the other parts and pieces. For handguns, it is usually made of brass or aluminum.

CCW: Long-time acronym meaning concealed carry permit; stands for concealed carry weapon. Is being replaced by the term CHL, which is more explanatory.

centerfire: A round with a primer cup located in the center of the flat bottom of the case.

chamber: The rear part of the barrel where a round comes to rest before it is fired. A revolver employs a multi-chambered rotating cylinder separated from the stationary barrel.

CHL: Common name for a concealed carry permit. It stands for concealed handgun license. Used interchangeably with CCW.

clear: To make certain a gun is unloaded or fix a malfunction so that the gun is ready to fire again.

clip: Often used to describe a magazine that stores and feeds ammunition (but the two are not synonymous). A clip feeds ammunition into a rifle and is then disposed of, while a magazine is reusable and typically an integral part of the firearm.

cock: The term referring to the action of manually drawing the hammer back until it latches in place, in preparation for its release, which occurs when you pull the trigger. Double-action external hammers—and all internal, or double-action only, hammers—may be cocked simply by pulling the trigger.

cocked and locked: 1911-style guns are typically carried cocked and locked, which means the hammer is cocked and the safety is on.

concealed: Hidden from view. A handgun is concealed when it is not discernable either through a direct view or through seeing the outline of the weapon through clothing (called "printing").

course of fire: A predetermined sequence of events in a shooting exercise.

cross dominance: When you are right-handed but left-eye dominant, or vice versa.

crown: The area inside the bore near the muzzle. Damage to the crown can severely impact a firearm's accuracy.

cylinder: A rotating cartridge holder in a revolver. Cartridges are held in chambers as the cylinder turns with each cock of the hammer, either to the left or to the right, lining up each chamber with the barrel/bore and the hammer or firing pin.

decocker: On double-action semi-automatic firearms, a lever that lowers the hammer without firing the gun.

dominant eye: The eye you use to aim with. Usually the same as your dominant hand—but not always.

dominant hand: The hand you write with.

double-action (DA): A type of firearm that may be discharged either by manually cocking the hammer and then pulling the trigger or by using the trigger to both cock and fire the weapon.

double-action only (DAO): A firearm in which the firing mechanism cannot be cocked for single-action use. Firing always occurs as a double-action sequence, where pulling the trigger both cocks and then fires the gun, as with a Ruger LCR or a Smith & Wesson Airweight.

double-action/single-action (DA/SA): A type of semi-automatic firearm that is designed to operate in double action on the first shot—with a long, heavy trigger pull—and in single action, with a lighter trigger pull, on all subsequent shots.

double tap: Two shots fired in rapid succession, generally without getting a new sight picture on the target.

downrange: The part of the range forward of the firing line, which is considered a safe direction to point the muzzle whenever you are on the range.

drop safety: A mechanical safety that prevents the gun from firing when it is unintentionally dropped.

dry fire: The operation of a firearm without the use of ammunition, as a means of gaining familiarity and skill. Dry firing is very beneficial, as long as you are certain the gun is unloaded.

dud: A round of ammunition that does not fire (as in a misfire).

dummy round (also called a snap cap): An inert, ammunition-shaped object, used in practice to simulate misfeeds and other malfunctions, and also used in dry-fire practice.

earmuffs: Hearing protection that completely covers both ears and is usually attached to a headband.

ear plugs: Hearing protection that fits inside the ear canal.

ears: Slang for all hearing protection, whether muffs or plugs. Range officers and trainers will often issue the command "ears on" before firing begins.

ejection port: The opening through which the empty, spent ammunition case is ejected from the breech of a firearm.

ejector: A piece of metal that ejects spent ammunition cases from a semi-automatic handgun.

ejector rod: The sliding metal dowel located in the middle of a revolver cylinder. After firing, the shooter opens the cylinder and depresses the front end of the ejection rod, which forces the hot, empty cases out of the cylinder.

electronic hearing protection: Earmuff hearing protection, such as that made by the Howard Leight company, that has internal electronics that amplifiy human voices while minimizing all noises louder than a specific decibel rating.

external manual safety: A safety lever found on the outer surfaces of the firearm, typically located on the upper back of a gun. This type of safety must be set and released by the shooter.

extractor: The piece of the pistol that pulls the spent cartridge case from the chamber as the slide slaps open, so it can be tossed out the ejection port by the ejector.

factory ammo: Ammunition that has been assembled by a commercial manufacturer and sold in retail stores, typically of a more consistent and higher quality (and subjected to higher standards) than reloads or hand loads assembled by an individual. Most new shooters should stick with factory ammo, in order to minimize the potential for any ammunition malfunctions.

feed ramp: A polished piece of metal which guides the ammunition up into the chamber.

firearm: A rifle, shotgun, or handgun using gunpowder as a propellant—by federal definition, under the 1968 Gun Control Act.

firing line: A line, either imaginary or marked, from which people fire their guns downrange at targets.

firing pin: A needle-like metal part of a modern firearm that strikes the primer, thereby initiating the firing of the cartridge.

firing pin block: A type of internal safety that prevents the firing pin from moving forward for any reason until and unless the trigger is pulled.

flinch: Pushing the gun downward just before firing, in an effort to compensate for the anticipated recoil. The main reason many new shooters shoot low. Can be minimized by trying a larger gun or lower caliber (or both).

follower: The follower in a magazine is the section of metal or plastic that rests atop the taut spring and helps to push the round up into the chamber (up the feed ramp).

follow-through: Holding the trigger to the rear after the shot has fired, until the sights are back on target, at which time the trigger is released until it resets and then is repulled to fire the next shot.

frame: The torso of the gun—the part off which all other parts hang.

front sight: The front sight is located at the muzzle end of the barrel. It is a blade-like raised surface that may have a dot or a fiber-optic tube, or may be the same color as the gun. To attain a proper sight picture and shoot with the greatest degree of accuracy, the shooter's eye should focus only on the front sight while shooting, allowing both the rear sight and the target to remain blurry.

front strap: The part of a revolver or pistol grip frame that faces forward and connects to the trigger guard.

grain: A unit of weight measurement used for bullets and gunpowder. The more grains, the heavier the bullet. Powder is also measured in grains, but this would apply only to shooters who reload ammunition. There are seven thousand grains to a pound.

grip: The handle used to hold a handgun. Also refers to the side panels of the handle or the method by which the shooter holds the handgun.

grip panels: The interchangeable surfaces that are installed on the part of the gun that you hold. Users may change grip panels to improve the look or feel of the firearm, or to personalize them so that the gun is more suited to a different hand size. Some grip panels are chosen for function, while others are chosen for looks. Common grip-panel materials are wood, plastic, and rubber.

grip safety: A passive, external safety typically located on the back strap, which must be fully depressed to release the trigger. Most 1911-style pistols feature a grip safety, as do Springfield XD models.

gunpowder: Chemical substances of various compositions, particle sizes, shapes, and colors that act as a propellant upon ignition. Ignited smokeless powder emits minimal quantities of smoke from a gun's muzzle, while traditional black powder can emit large quantities of whitish smoke.

hammer: The part of the pistol that, when activated by the trigger or by manual cocking, is released to fall forward and strike a firing pin or, when the firing pin is attached to the hammer, strike the primer cup itself and discharge the weapon. Hammers are found on both semi-autos and revolvers, though not all guns have hammers. Many guns are equipped with strikers—notably Glock pistols. Hammers may be exposed or shrouded, spurred or bobbed.

hammerless: A revolver or pistol design, typically for concealed carry purposes, that actually has hammers that are fully encased inside the frames, or where the spurs have been removed or dramatically reduced to prevent snagging.

hammer spur: The thumbpiece on the top rear of the hammer that enables it to be manually cocked.

handgun: Synonym for pistol. A handgun is designed to be held aloft in one or two hands, versus being braced against the shoulder as a rifle or shotgun would be.

hollow-point: A bullet with a hollow nose that mushrooms or expands when it strikes a sold target. Commonly used for self-defense, hollow-points are less likely to overpenetrate the target and harm an innocent bystander.

holster: A gun holder that may be strapped to the body, attached to the inside of a purse or bag, or dropped into a pocket. A holster serves to protect the gun's finish and provide security by covering the trigger so it cannot be pulled accidentally, and to present the grip of the gun at a constant angle for easy access. Pocket holsters also serve to obscure the outline of the gun so it does not print. Holsters may be made from cloth, leather, suede, or plastic.

internal safety: A safety that is located inside the gun and is not accessible to the user. Internal safeties are designed to prevent unintentional discharges when the gun is dropped or mishandled.

Isosceles stance: A shooting stance in which the gun is held straight out from the body, with both arms straight and both legs straight, each forming an isosceles triangle.

jam: A malfunction that locks up the gun and prevents it from firing properly.

kick: Slang for recoil.

Kydex: A composite that combines the beneficial characteristics of acrylic and PVC with rigidity and formability; it is also tough, chemical resistant, and resilient. Used in a variety of holsters.

lands: The raised portions of the bore between the grooves of the rifling. The top surface of the lands is approximately the same diameter as the bore was prior to rifling.

laser grip: A grip that contains a pressure-activated laser pointer, enabling the shooter to quickly and accurately aim the firearm.

laser sight: An alternative sighting device that projects a laser onto an object to assist with aiming. The laser allows a shooter to quickly and accurately see where the firearm is aimed, even when low light prevents using the gun's normal sights. Lasers may be located within the grips, hung from accessory rails at the front end of the gun, wrapped around the trigger guard, or built into the firearm. A laser can be helpful but should never replace pulling the trigger. Too many people want to depend on the laser to frighten an intruder, which is unlikely.

LC: Long Colt, a type of ammunition.

length of pull: The distance the trigger must travel before it breaks, thus firing the gun.

LEO: Law enforcement officer.

limp-wristing: A soft wrist, which is buffeted and controlled by the gun's recoil, usually creating the potential for stovepipes and poor target patterns.

loaded: The condition of a firearm that has ammunition in its chamber, cylinder, or magazine.

loaded chamber indicator: A part of the gun that protrudes or pops up when a round is in the chamber ready to be fired, giving a visual and tactile indication that the gun is loaded. On a Springfield XD or a Ruger LC9, the loaded chamber indicator is a metal bar that pops up from the top of the gun.

long trigger: A trigger that must be pulled for a long time before it breaks.

LR: Long Rifle, as in .22 Long Rifle ammunition.

magazine: A container, typically detachable in handguns, that holds cartridges under spring pressure for feeding into the gun's chamber. Magazines may be double-stack or single-stack, with the double-stack variation holding more rounds than single-stack. The total number of rounds held by a magazine is referred to as the "magazine capacity."

magazine pouch: Commonly shortened to mag pouch, this is a device to hold extra magazines, which fastens to the shooter's belt.

mag loader: Sometimes erroneously called an autoloader or speed loader. A mechanical device that makes it easier to fill magazines using less hand strength and without hurting one's fingertips or thumbs.

Magnum: A term indicating a relatively heavily loaded metallic cartridge. It generally indicates a round that cannot be interchanged with other rounds of the same caliber (for example, a .22 Magnum round cannot be fired in a firearm chambered for .22 Long Rifle ammunition).

mag release button: Normally located beside the trigger guard (sometimes on the left side of the gun, sometimes on both sides—which is referred to as an ambidextrous or "ambi" mag release), this button, when depressed, allows the magazine to drop free. On Walther guns, the mag release is a lever located on the trigger guard, and on many European models, the mag release is located on the butt of the grip.

mag safety (also called magazine disconnect): A device that prevents the gun from being able to fire when the magazine is removed from the gun, even if there is a round in the chamber.

mag well: The opening in the bottom of the gun into which a magazine is fed. On a semi-auto handgun, the magazine well is at the base of the grip.

manual safety: A safety that the shooter must manually turn off or on before or after firing the gun. The most common form of safety mechanism is a lever, which, when set to the safe position, prevents the trigger from being pullable.

match grade: A higher quality item used to increase accuracy—generally used for competition in a match. Match-grade ammo and barrels are the most common improvements made to a firearm to improve accuracy for competition.

misfeed: Failure of the next round to completely enter the chamber. Misfeeds and failures to feed are very similar; a failure to feed is a round that is never stripped off the top of the magazine, while a misfeed is a round that leaves the magazine but does not properly enter the chamber.

misfire: The condition of a cartridge not firing when an attempt to fire it is made. It can be caused by either a defective cartridge or a defective firearm. The term is frequently misused to indicate a negligent discharge of a firearm.

moon clip: A flat, circular loading device for revolvers that is designed specifically for rimless cartridges (such as 9mm Luger or .45 ACP); it becomes an integral part of the revolver while firing.

muzzle: The open end of the barrel from which the bullet exits when the gun is fired.

muzzle blast: The noise and concussion that results when hot gasses pour out of the barrel after the bullet clears the muzzle.

muzzle control: Being alert to the direction your firearm is pointed at all times, and always keeping it pointed in a safe direction.

muzzle velocity: The speed of the bullet, measured in feet per second, as it leaves the barrel.

night sights: A type of sight, often in the three-dot style, that glows yellow-green in the dark. Some night sights are made of tritium, a radioactive substance, while others use a phosphorus paint.

NRA: The National Rifle Association. This organization coordinates shooting events at the national level, lobbies for pro-gun legislation, and provides firearms training to civilians and law enforcement, as well as supporting Americans' Second Amendment right to carry firearms.

open carry: A legal definition that permits law-abiding citizens to carry exposed weapons, without seeking any kind of special permit to do so.

out of battery: A semi-automatic is said to be out of battery when the slide fails to come all the way forward again after the gun has fired. This condition can be created by a misfeed, a dirty gun, weak springs, the shooter's thumbs brushing against the slide, riding the slide, or any of several other causes.

over-travel: If the trigger can continue moving to the rear after the shot has fired, the trigger is said to have over-traveled.

+P ammunition: Ammunition that has been loaded to a higher internal pressure than is typical for its caliber. Many older calibers are available in both standard and +P or +P+ variants. Ammunition marked +P produces more power and higher pressure than the standard ammunition. Not all firearms are approved for increased pressure; check your owner's manual before loading +P or +P+ rounds.

pattern: The relationship of hits on a target. The closer together, the better the pattern. A tight pattern is one in which the hits are closely grouped when they land on the target. A loose pattern is one in which they are widely spread.

pistol: Synonymous with handgun, this can mean either a revolver or a semi-auto.

plinking: Casual shooting at paper targets. The most common shooting sport in the United States.

port: An opening. The ejection port is the opening in the side of a semi-auto from which spent cases are ejected.

powder: See *gunpowder.*

powder charge: The amount of propellant powder that is suitable for specific cartridge/bullet combinations.

primer: A small metal cup that contains a tiny explosive charge that is sensitive to impact. It is detonated by the striking of a firing pin in the firearm. On a rimfire handgun, the primer is not located in a cup but is placed around the rim of the cartridge.

printing: When the outline of a concealed handgun is discernable through the clothing.

propellant: In a firearm, the chemical composition (often referred to as powder or gunpowder) that is detonated by the primer.

pull: The entire process of moving the trigger backward until it breaks and then allowing it to reset.

pull distance: The distance the trigger must travel before it breaks and fires the gun.

racking the slide: Also called charging the weapon. Pulling the slide back to its rearmost position, and then letting it slap forward. Racking the slide loads the chamber and prepares the gun for firing.

rail/tactical rail: Located beneath the barrel, attached to the frame, this feature allows for the attachment of accessories such as laser or tactical lights.

rails: The metal surfaces of a semi-auto slide that are the part of the frame upon which the slide moves forward and backward.

reach: The distance from the back strap to the front of the trigger.

reactive targets: Targets that respond somehow when you hit them, such as exploding, falling, or releasing smoke.

rear sight: Located at the back of the barrel closest to the shooter. It is typically two dots with a notch in the middle, designed to be visually placed on either side of the front sight while shooting, although it can also be a single dot, a *U*, a *V*, or a ring or some other configuration.

recoil: Often referred to as the kick, this is the rearward force against the shooter when a firearm is fired. This force is due to Newton's third law of physics (for every action there is an equal and opposite reaction). The heavier the bullet and the faster it leaves the muzzle of the barrel, the greater the recoil. Recoil can be lessened by a larger, heavier gun or a lighter round.

recoil spring: The spring that cushions the slide in its rearward travel and then sends the slide forward again with enough force to drive a new round into the chamber.

reset: The point during the release of the trigger pull when the gun's internal mechanisms are ready to fire again.

revolver: Handgun, typically, with a multi-chambered cylinder that rotates to individually align each chamber with a single barrel and the hammer/firing pin.

ride the slide: Racking the slide incorrectly by allowing your hand to rest upon the slide as it moves forward during the loading procedure. Riding the slide is a common cause of misfeeds and other malfunctions.

rifling: Spiral grooves (known as lands and grooves) in a gun's bore that spin the bullet in flight and improve accuracy.

rimfire: A type of firearm cartridge. It is called a rimfire because instead of the firing pin of a gun striking the primer cup at the center of the base of the cartridge to ignite it (as in a centerfire cartridge), the pin strikes the base's rim. A rimmed or flanged cartridge with the priming mixture located inside the rim of the case. The most famous example is the .22 rimfire.

rimless: A cartridge in which the base diameter is the same as the body diameter. The casing will normally have an extraction groove machined around it near the base, creating a rim at the base that is the same diameter as the body diameter.

round: Synonym for a cartridge. A unit of measure for ammunition that is one complete unit of ammunition—including a bullet (or other projectile), powder, and a primer—and is contained in an outer shell or case. Typical quantities are twenty rounds and fifty rounds in a single box.

round nose or ball tip: The classic bullet shape.

safety: A mechanical device used to block the firing pin or trigger such that the firearm cannot be fired.

sear: The part of the trigger mechanism that holds the hammer or striker back. Pressure on the trigger causes the sear to release the hammer or striker, allowing it to strike the firing pin and discharge the weapon.

Second Amendment: The second article in the United States Bill of Rights, which states, "A well-regulated militia being necessary to the security of a free state, the right of the people to keep and bear arms shall not be infringed."

semi-automatic: A firearm designed to fire a single cartridge, eject the empty case, and reload the chamber each time the trigger is pulled. It uses the energy from the fired shot to eject the empty case and feed the next round into the chamber.

semi-wadcutter (SWC): A bullet design featuring a conical extended nose with a flat point and a sharp-edged shoulder that serves to cut a full diameter hole in the target. This design also may be found with a hollow-point to facilitate expansion. The modified wadcutter bullet design, with slightly sloping edges, is designed to load smoothly in a semi-automatic pistol.

short trigger: A trigger that doesn't have to travel very far before it reaches the break. In a 1911 semi-auto pistol, a short trigger is a different part than a long trigger, and (in addition to providing less motion) it features a shorter reach, which may be of benefit to a small-handed shooter.

sight alignment: The manner in which the sights are lined up properly in front of the shooter's eye, to form a straight path to the target.

sight, front: See *front sight*

sight picture: What the shooter sees when looking through the sights at the target.

sight radius: The distance between the rear sight and the front sight.

sight, rear: See *rear sight*

sights: The devices that aid the eye in aiming the barrel of a firearm in the proper direction to hit a target. They can be mechanical, optical, or electronic. Iron sights, sometimes known as open sights, consist of specially shaped pieces of metal placed at each end of the barrel. The sight closest to the muzzle end of the gun is called the front sight, while the one farthest from the muzzle (and nearest to the shooter) is called the rear sight.

single-action (SA): A handgun whose trigger performs only one (single) task—releasing the hammer. On single-action revolvers, the shooter uses a thumb to draw back the hammer (that is, cock it) before each shot. On single-action pistols, the movement of the slide backwards will recock the hammer for subsequent shots. The hammer may be cocked by hand, by racking the slide, or by the rearward movement of the slide after each shot is fired. The most widely known single-action semi-auto handgun is the 1911-style pistol designed by John Moses Browning. Today, such guns as the Sig Sauer P938 and the Sig P238 are also single-action. Single-action pistols tend to have a lighter, more comfortable trigger pull because the trigger is not performing two tasks.

slide: The hard metal sheath that covers the barrel and contains the breechblock and parts of the firing mechanism. As you fire the gun, the slide moves back and forth rapidly, ejecting the spent casings and loading a new round into the chamber.

slide lock: When a semi-automatic gun has been fired until the magazine is empty, the slide will lock open—that is, remain in its farthest back position so that you can see into the breech. This is called "slide lock."

slide release: The slide release lever is usually located on the left side of the slide and is pushed down to unlock the slide and release it to move forward into its normal position. It is also called the slide stop.

small arms: Guns designed to be carried—that is, pistols or revolvers.

smokeless powder: The propellant used in modern ammunition. Unlike black powder, it is not explosive but burns rapidly and creates a large volume of gas. It is today's version of gunpowder and is usually made from nitrocellulose, or a blend of nitrocellulose and nitroglycerin.

snap cap: A plastic faux ammunition piece, used in dry-fire practice to cushion the firing pin as it strikes.

speed loader: In revolvers, a circular device that contains a complete set of cartridges and can be inserted into all chambers of the cylinder simultaneously. This term is also used for devices that assist with the loading of semi-automatic magazines.

spotting scope: A magnification device for looking downrange and judging how close the shooter's bullets were to the target or bull's-eye. Permits longer distance shooting, without the necessity of walking back and forth to the target.

squib load: A round of ammunition that does not have sufficient power to reach the target downrange, or, sometimes, to even exit the barrel. Squib loads are very uncommon when shooting modern factory ammo.

stance: Your position while shooting—that is, how you hold your feet, hips, arms, and shoulders—as in the Weaver or Isosceles stances.

stopping power: A much-used but oft-misunderstood term related to a gun's ability to prevent an assailant from advancing. In reality, stopping power is dictated more by bullet placement than by the type of gun or ammo involved.

stovepipe: A spent casing that lodges itself upright in the ejection port because it has failed to clear the closing slide in time. Typically caused by limp-wristing during firing or by a dirty or unoiled gun.

striker: A forward-moving, spring-loaded rod that strikes the primer of a chambered cartridge.

takedown lever: The lever or switch on many semi-automatics that allows you to initiate the process of disassembling the gun.

tap, rack, bang: The slang term for the procedure to clear a misfeed. To clear a misfeed, tap the base of the magazine firmly to be sure it is properly seated, rack the slide to eject an empty case or feed a new round, and assess to be sure your target still needs shooting. If it does, pull the trigger to create the bang.

thumb safety: An external manual safety, usually located just below or on the slide at the rear of the gun, allowing it to be engaged or disengaged with your dominant thumb.

top strap: The part of a revolver frame that extends over the top of the cylinder and connects the top of the standing breech with the forward portion of the frame into which the barrel is mounted.

transfer bar: When the trigger is pulled, the transfer bar moves into a position that "transfers" the impact of the hammer strike to the firing pin. A blow to the uncocked hammer cannot cause a discharge because the transfer bar is not in position and cannot transfer the force to the firing pin.

trigger: The release device that allows a gun to fire. When a trigger is pulled, it releases a striker or a hammer, causing the firing pin to strike the primer. The primer then ignites the propellant (smokeless powder) within the round. Hot gas from the powder expands the brass or aluminum case, pushing the bullet down the barrel so that it exits the muzzle. A trigger may either release (single-action) or cock and release (double-action) a hammer, as well as rotating a revolver's cylinder and releasing internal safeties.

trigger control: A smooth pull, with the pad of your finger (not the first joint) on the trigger, and the appropriate follow-through by realigning the sights and allowing the trigger to reset before you pull again.

trigger group: The moving parts that work together to fire the gun when the trigger is pulled. This may include trigger springs, the trigger, the sear, disconnectors, and other parts.

trigger guard: A flat band of metal or plastic that wraps around the trigger to protect it from being jiggled or pulled. You should never place your finger within the guard or on the trigger itself until you are ready to shoot.

trigger lock: A locking device that, when used on a firearm, makes it impossible to fire. Federal law requires that every new gun sold must be accompanied by a trigger lock.

trigger safety: Often a blade located in the middle of a trigger (as on Glocks and Springfield XDs) or a segmented trigger (as on Smith & Wesson M&Ps), which prevents the trigger from being accidentally depressed by foreign objects brushing against it.

trigger weight: The amount of pressure required to pull the trigger past its break point.

wadcutter (WC): A round that has a flat end and is used mostly in competition because it cuts a very clean, round hole in paper for scoring purposes.

weapon: Any tool that can be used to apply or project lethal force. Webster defines it as "an instrument of offensive or defensive combat."

Weaver stance: A shooting position named for Deputy Sheriff Jack Weaver, who defined the stance based on how a boxer stands when in a fight. The body is angled slightly in relation to the target, with elbows flexed slightly. The strong-side arm pushes out, while the weak hand pulls back. This produces a push-pull tension.

wheel gun: Another term for a revolver.

MAJOR PISTOL MANUFACTURERS

Beretta: www.beretta.com

Bersa: www.bersa.com

Colt: www.colt.com

Glock: us.glock.com

Kahr Arms: www.kahr.com

Kel-Tec Firearms: www.keltecweapons.com

Kimber: www.kimberamerica.com

Ruger: www.ruger.com

Sig Sauer: www.sigsauer.com

Smith & Wesson: www.smith-wesson.com

Springfield: www.springfield-armory.com

Walther: www.waltherarms.com

VALUABLE LINKS
FOR EDUCATION AND ENLIGHTENMENT

Girl's Guide to Guns: www.girlsguidetoguns.com

Gun Owners of America: www.gunowners.org/

Gunsite (training academy started by Col. Jeff Cooper): www.gunsite.com

National Rifle Association: www.nra.org

National Shooting Sports Foundation: www.nssf.org

NRA gun laws: www.nraila.org/gun-laws.aspx

Second Amendment Foundation: www.saf.org

Students for Concealed Carry: www.concealedcampus.org

United States Concealed Carry Association: www.usconcealedcarry.com/

The Well Armed Woman—"Where the Feminine and Firearms Meet": www.thewellarmedwoman.com

Women & Guns: www.womenshooters.com

GUN LAW INFORMATION

FOR ALL FIFTY STATES, GUAM, AND US VIRGIN ISLANDS

Alabama: www.ago.state.al.us/Page-Gun-Reprocity-Law

Alaska: www.dps.alaska.gov/Statewide/PermitsLicensing/default.aspx

Arizona: www.azdps.gov/Services/Concealed_Weapons/

Arkansas: www.asp.arkansas.gov/services-and-programs/detail/ concealed-handgun-licensing

California: www.oag.ca.gov/firearms

Colorado: www.colorado.gov/pacific/csp/colorado-gun-laws

Connecticut: www.ct.gov/despp/cwp/view.asp?a=4213&Q=530224&despp Nav_GID=2080

Delaware: www.courts.delaware.gov/Superior/weapons.stm

Florida: www.freshfromflorida.com/Divisions-Offices/Licensing/ Concealed-Weapon-License

Georgia: www.georgiaconcealedcarry.com/georgia-state-gun-laws/

Guam: www.gpd.guam.gov/faq/

Hawaii: www.hawaiiccw.com/hawaii-gun-firearm-laws/

Idaho: www.ag.idaho.gov/concealedWeapons/concealedWeapons_index.html

Illinois: www.isp.state.il.us/docs/ptfire.pdf

Indiana: www.in.gov/isp/firearms.htm

Iowa: www.dps.state.ia.us/asd/weapon_permits.shtml

Kansas: www.ag.ks.gov/public-safety/concealedcarry

Kentucky: www.kentuckystatepolice.org/ccdw/conceal.html

Louisiana: www.lsp.org/handguns.html

Maine: www.maine.gov/dps/msp/licenses/weapons_permits.html

Maryland: www.mdsp.org/Organization/SupportServicesBureau/ LicensingDivision/MainLicensingPage.aspx

Massachusetts: www.mass.gov/eopss/firearms-reg-and-laws/

Michigan: www.michigan.gov/msp/0,1607,7-123-1591_3503_4654---,00.html

Minnesota: www.dps.mn.gov/divisions/bca/bca-divisions/administrative/Pages/firearms.aspx

Mississippi: www.dps.state.ms.us/firearms/firearms-permit-unit/

Missouri: www.handgunlaw.us/states/missouri.pdf

Montana: www.dojmt.gov/enforcement/concealed-weapons/

Nebraska: www.statepatrol.nebraska.gov/ConcealedCarry.aspx

Nevada: www.leg.state.nv.us/NRs/NRS-202.html#NRS202Sec3689

New Hampshire: www.nh.gov/safety/divisions/nhsp/ssb/permitslicensing/plupr.html

New Jersey: www.nj.gov/oag/services_arms.htm

New Mexico: www.dps.state.nm.us/

New York: www.troopers.ny.gov/Firearms/

New York City: www.nyc.gov/html/nypd/html/permits/permits.shtml

North Carolina: www.ncdoj.com/getdoc/19be6294-bfbf-4875-bbef-ac2ebb6f47b2/2-6-3-6-3-Concealed-Weapon-Reciprocity.aspx

North Dakota: www.ag.nd.gov/BCI/CW/CW.htm

Ohio: www.ohioattorneygeneral.gov/Law-Enforcement/Concealed-Carry

Oklahoma: www.ok.gov/osbi/Handgun_Licensing/index.html

Oregon: www.orcgon.gov/OSP/ID/pagcs/chl.aspx

Pennsylvania: www.attorneygeneral.gov/Media_and_Resources/Firearm_Reciprocity_Agreements/

Rhode Island: http://webserver.rilin.state.ri.us/Statutes/TITLE11/11-47/INDEX.HTM

South Carolina: www.sled.sc.gov/cwp.aspx?MenuID=CWP

South Dakota: https://sdsos.gov/services-for-individuals/concealed-pistol-permits/default.aspx

Tennessee: www.tn.gov/safety/handgunmainarticle/

Texas: www.txdps.state.tx.us/rsd/chl/

US Virgin Islands: www.vipd.gov.vi/Departments/Office_of_the_Police_Commissioner/Firearms_Unit.aspx

Utah: http://bci.utah.gov/concealed-firearm/

Vermont: www.ago.vermont.gov/divisions/criminal-division/gun-laws.php

Virginia: www.vsp.state.va.us/Firearms.shtm

Washington: www.dol.wa.gov/business/firearms/falaws.html

West Virginia: www.ago.wv.gov/gunreciprocity/Pages/default.aspx

Wisconsin: www.doj.state.wi.us/dles/cib/conceal-carry/concealed-carry

Wyoming: http://wyomingdci.wyo.gov/dci-criminal-justice-information-systems-section/concealed-firearms-permits

INDEX

ejection rod, 56
expectations, 35
eye protection, 116
eyes
    dominant, 117–118
    keeping open, 36–37, 155

fanny packs, 153
fear, 16–17, 29, 78
Federal Hydra-Shok, 106
feed ramp, 66
fieldstripping process, 132
firing pin, 62
fit, 84–89
Flashbang Holster, 152
flinching, 127
floating barrel, 66–67
follow through, 127
frame, 61
front sight, 59
front strap, 59, 63

garter holster, 152
Glock, 70–71, 81, 85, 92, 133
    42, 36, 81–82
    43, 81–82
    Gen 3, 75
    Gen 4, 75, 76
grains per round, 106
grip, 59, 63, 67, 71–76,
    119–122
grip panel, 59, 74
guide rod, 132
Gun Box RFID, 141
gun safes, 139–141
gun shops, 93, 159–163

hammer, 59, 61–62, 63–64,
    90, 91
*Handgun Wounding Factors
    and Effectiveness* (FBI),
    102–103
hangfire, 108–109
Hatcher's Notebook, 45–46
hearing protection, 46–47,
    116–117
Heritage Rough Rider,
    70, 89
hollow-points, 102–107
holsters, 144–145, 149–153
home safety, 25–27

Hoppe's No. 9 (bore solvent),
    134, 136
Hornady
    Critical Defense, 105–106
    Critical Duty, 105–106
    One Shot, 136, 137
Howard Leight company,
    117
hunters, 42

insurance, 168
Isosceles stance, 123–124,
    125

Kel-Tec
    P-3AT, 50–51, 152
    P-11, 83, 138–139
    PF-9, 91
kick (recoil), 20, 21, 33, 35
Kimber Ultra Carry, 90
Kydex Blackhawk locking
    holster, 145

lands and grooves, 60–61
lasers, 38–40
laws, state, 29, 115, 147–149,
    155–156
loading ammunition, 111
loading gate, 59, 60

magazine, 52, 54, 59, 67–69,
    72, 73–74, 111
magazine release, 59, 67
magazine safety, 68–69
Magnum Research, 72
manual safety, 70
misfire, 108–109
mothers, 38
muzzle, 59
muzzle direction, 45–48
muzzle flip, 33

names, 81
National Shooting Sports
    Foundation (NSSF), 93
natural aim point, 37–38
911, 28
noise-attenuating muffs, 117
North American Arms, 20

oil, 137, 138
open carry, 29–30

penetration, 101, 104
permanent cavity wound,
    101, 104
personal defense
    aim and, 37–38
    ammunition for, 102–105
    Castle Doctrine and,
        168–169
    example of, 25–30
    wound types and, 101
+P, 100–102
+P+, 102
pocket carry, 114–115
police
    calling, 30
    interactions with, 86,
        155–156
    role of, 165–166
primer cup, 98

radio frequency
    identification (RFID), 141
range
    indoor, 125–126
    outdoor, 126
    shooting at, 127–129
    standard operating
        procedures at, 116,
        125–126
    unsolicited advice at, 114
range safety officers (RSOs),
    114, 125
recoil (kick), 20, 21, 33, 35
release buttons, 50–51, 53
retailers. *See* gun shops
revolvers, 17, 58–65, 79–81
rifling, 60
Rig-Rag, 135
rimfire ammunition, 98–99
round-nose ammunition, 99
Ruger
    LC9, 83, 91
    LCP, 65, 152
    LCR, 53, 80, 81, 91
    Single-Six, 89
    SP101, 64
    SR 22, 73, 74, 85, 133
Ruger Blackhawk, 89

safe-action, 92–93

ACKNOWLEDGMENTS

Layne English for her time and talent in getting the cover photo shot!

Courtney Meyers for being a patient and beautiful model (and for being a "gun girl" herself!).

Vandalia Range & Armory for assistance with products and allowing me to photograph (and shoot in) their lovely indoor range.